*F*ashion
*F*ood
&
*F*orget-Me-Nots

Kathryne Hays

Published by
LaGrange College

FIRST EDITION
1993

LIBRARY OF CONGRESS CATALOG CARD NUMBER: 93-77798

For Jane,
    I just love
your Mother, so
I'm sure I'll like
you.
            Love and happiness,
                Kathryn

February 1993

Kathryne Hays, known by her friends as Kay, was born in Madison, Georgia. She completed her A.B. and B.S. degrees at LaGrange College and immediately went to work at DuPont as a research chemist. She then started her own cosmetic company, The House of Hays. After deciding that her real interest was in the fashion industry, she joined Bamberger's as Associate Fashion Coordinator. She caught the attention of the management at *Vogue* magazine and was offered an editorial position, soon becoming the shoe editor. She later became Director of Accessories and was promoted to Senior Editor in 1983.

During the 38 years she worked at *Vogue*, she traveled to many countries seeking new ideas that would contribute to her professional search for better fashions in women's wear, and she received many notable awards. The Italian government recognized her for introducing Italian shoes in American fashions. The knitwear industry has honored her for her work with DuPont in manufacturing colored stockings. The Fashion Footwear Industry presented Kay in 1990 the Lifetime Achievement Award.

In recognition of her excellence in artistic achievement and her many contributions to fashion in America, the trustees and faculty of LaGrange College conferred upon her the Degree of Doctor of Humane Letters in June of 1992. While Kay's forte' has been the pursuit of excellence in her profession, she has remained a caring human being interested in other people, offering them a helping hand along the way.

Walter Y. Murphy

Dr. Walter Y. Murphy
President of LaGrange College

February 1993

In 1953, I first heard of Kay Hays. I have kept up with her many successes ever since. I knew she was a brilliant, creative business woman who had traveled to over a hundred countries during her illustrious career with *Vogue* magazine. When I finally met her, I found her to be a warm, generous, down-to-earth person who is loyal to her friends and who is a lover of music, animals and nature. Her laughter is heart warming and her stories, mostly personal experiences, are priceless!

We, at LaGrange College, are proud to claim this unique individual as one of our own. She inspires all students to set their goals high and to strive for excellence in all things.

Marianne Murphy

Marianne Murphy

Dedicated to Jessica Daves and Armi Ratia
Neither one is still with us
except in the hearts of
those who knew and loved them.

Kay Hays

FOREWORD

I feel like a child in a candy store to be able to write the way I choose and to say whatever I like. During my professional life of more than 45 years, I have written volumes of work but usually there have been restrictions— things one must not say, limitations — nothing too personal.

This book is me with all the warts showing. It isn't about me, but I haven't protected my feelings.

I waited until I was almost 68 to write a book, so it seemed I should say what came naturally. Before it is finished I may have second thoughts, and wish I had been more reserved — but so be it.

Basically the book is about love — love for one's environment and those who inhabit it, human, animal and vegetable. It's about aging, growing (I hope), sharing and enjoying. It's about inhaling deeply the aromas of good food, flowers, friendship and being glad.

K-N.

TABLE OF CONTENTS

Looking Over One Shoulder

I have lived in New York City for more than forty years and even today there are those who insist that I still have a strong hint of a Southern accent. It is unlikely that I should have become literate, learned to spell, and most of all, be able to separate my language from the colloquialisms that spiced my early days.

My childhood was spent in a small, beautiful and historic Southern town in central Georgia called Madison, the county seat of Morgan County. This lovely old town was one of the few that was not destroyed in the Civil War so that the high ceilinged colonial homes with walk-in windows, boxwood gardens, azalea, crepe myrtle, wisteria, magnolia trees and oversized oak trees that met overhead, almost covering the sky, still existed and we lived happily with them.

The best part of my early days was my close association and friendship with my black friends. They added spice, colorful language, warmth and love to my childhood. They taught me to sing the blues, to tell it like they wanted it to be (honest but somewhat exaggerated and always with a happy ending). Both have stayed with me all of my life. I don't even like unhappy words. Doom and gloom are not part of my vocabulary. My best friend was Charlie Helen Baldwin. It is not unusual for Southern families to name a girl after both parents. My name is Harvey Kathryne Hays. Something I have chosen to forget especially when I received numerous booklets from men's colleges. She and I went to our black friends' weddings and their Sunday evening church services. All the schools and churches were segregated at this time. We had strong friendships unspoiled by and unaware of color differences. The best part of me as a person came from these early friends. They taught me to keep my hand and heart close to the earth, the animals and the seductiveness of nature. The 2,500 population when I lived in Madison was made up equally of black and white people.

Charlie was my next door neighbor. She and I had a laughing, good childhood. We drank in the delights of growing up together, crossing back and forth from one yard to the other, sharing the intimacies of each new earth-shattering experience. A thick hedge

1

separated our two velvety grassed yards, but we had made the trip back and forth so often that we had an opening where we could slip through the heavy growth.

After school Charlie and I usually had, what we considered, an interesting and compelling project to fill our leisure hours. Those were times when we took a generous amount of junk food (an apple to please my mother) and Cokes and set off into the woods for an adventure. We always half hoped that we would get lost and feel really special. We never did.

One of the things we did that stays with me today was write a spoof of Shakespeare's *Merchant of Venice*. At the time of this literary endeavor we were around twelve years of age.

While we were doing our impish, humorous writing we stuck with the job most afternoons for several hours at a time. We used to write and laugh and laugh. It seems to me that we did finally complete the play, and that we were extremely pleased at our results; however, I don't remember that we were able to persuade anyone (other than ourselves) to read our amusing accomplishments. No matter, the doing and the completion were the name of the game.

Even at that early age my parents impressed upon me the need to finish what we started. Charlie and I were both very religious. We went to church twice on Sunday, prayer meeting on Wednesday evenings and to the youth meetings on Sunday evenings before the regular service. Both of us were members of the Methodist Church and I believe we both taught Sunday School when we were old enough to do so. Our special friend, Evelyn Stovall (now Bullock), played the piano beautifully, and naturally she played at the young people's meetings.

In the South there were two things that determined if you were a worthwhile, good person: One was that you must be a loyal church goer, and the other was that you must smile and speak to everyone you met. I've always been convinced that anyone in the South was considered a successful and a desirable person if *they* had the capacity to greet all comers with a "Good morning, how are you today?" and whenever possible, time permitting, to make a comment about the weather. When I came to New York City I found that someone could be committed for less.

At the time I thought that Charlie and I were two of the friendliest and most cheerful youths in Madison. We were so popular that when we graduated from Junior High School each of us received numerous gifts such as stockings and handkerchiefs from all our adult friends. Surely we must be worthwhile to have so many admirers. Our cup runneth over. Life was ours for the taking.

We knew little or nothing about what went on in the world outside of our town. The entire town was mostly Protestant. There was only one Jewish family in the village. Their home burned, and I persuaded my mother to invite the daughter (Doris Freedman who taught me speech in school) to stay with us until they had a new house. I loved having her. She was beautiful.

What a narrow, sheltered life we led. I didn't know what the word *prejudice* meant, and I hope that I still do not know. To me people are people to love and cherish. The differences make for more interesting friendships. It's these differences that have kept me attracted to New York City.

Madison gave me security, I knew every person who lived there and I felt loved. I belonged to my family and to my town. For many years, our house was across the street from the school, which is now a cultural center. Each morning my black and white fox terrier and I went to school. He returned home, but was always at the school to greet me when I came out to go home for lunch.

There was a girl in my fifth grade class who had ambitions to be our leader. I'll call her Dorothy. She was several years older than most of the class and a large, rough jewel of a country girl who used to chase me around the school in hopes of punching me in the nose. This would prove her physical superiority. Needless to say, I ran like mad and on the days I escaped I ran home at noon feeling relief for having temporarily side-stepped the ordeal. It was not unusual to open my front door and find Dorothy waiting to sock it to me. She was none too smart in her studies, but she was foxy enough to arrive early, tell my mother that she had stomach cramps (something she had several

3

times a month and my mother never saw through her scheme) and get invited for a hot meal. After Dorothy had punched me and I walked in with a bloody nose, my mother comforted me and asked what happened. Big bad Dorothy stood behind my five-foot-two mother with a clenched fist that said, "Don't you dare tell." So, of course, I explained that I just had a nose bleed.

Last year I invited Charlie Baldwin and Evelyn Stovall to my millhouse for a week. We had not seen each other for about forty-seven years, with the exception of seeing Evelyn the year before in 1984, and we talked and talked and laughed about our early years. One of the stories that the three of us remembered and were amused by was Dorothy's continued struggle to rule us.

The Garden Club of America has a pilgrimage each spring to Madison to see the old homes and gardens. I have been told by two friends who took the trip how much I would like this charming little town that had been completely preserved. Neither knew that it was my home town and that I lived there until I graduated from LaGrange College.

My restless Aquarian disposition, January 21st, was still strong and I had taken a double major at LaGrange, fine arts and science. The plan was to go to medical school. My junior year I became engaged to marry; so when I graduated in 1943 I had to decide whether to go to medical school or get married. During my junior year E.I. DuPont had offered me a job as a chemist in its research lab. My husband was going to Officer's Training School at Fort Monmouth, New Jersey. I chose marriage and took a job in the DuPont research labs in Arlington just across the river from New York City. They gave me time off to get married in November. We lived in upper Montclair until I could move to a village closer to Fort Monmouth and work in the research labs there while my husband was overseas.

I have continued to have a love affair with the simple life and to be attracted to the depth rather than the surface of a person. It has occurred to me that this small town background and curiosity for nature, for all living creatures, and the intrigue and fantasy of fashion served as a balance, a see-saw one for the other, adding strength and magic to my sensitivity.

4

As I get older, I find that the aesthetics of life attract me most. I have always been closely involved with music, art, sounds, smells, gardens, and animals. I almost became a folk singer and even spent two summers during my college years collecting and teaching folk songs in the Ozarks and the Dakotas.

The happiness of these earlier years served to cast beautiful shadows over my entire life. When I look back, I realize how blessed I am to have grown up with the shade of great trees to shelter me from the heat of life.

I was the youngest of four children. My only sister was eight years older and my two brothers ten and twelve years older than my sister, so I grew up almost as an only child. This made it necessary and possible for me to explore and make decisions on my own, and indulge my love of nature.

One of the strongest influences in my junior high years was a teacher, Eulalee Macdowell, who taught me to sight read first by the paragraph and then the page. This opened the world of literature to me. After my parents tucked me in, kissed me good night and wished me roses on my pillow, I would read a book three or four nights a week. They were checked out from the high school library and were seldom novels. I especially liked English literature. It was like a great hunger I could not fill. A thirst I could not quench. These books kindled my desire to travel. They made me aware. They taught me to observe, to absolve, to improvise. I could hardly wait for college. The first day I arrived, I brought my English literature book home and read it through the first night. My English professor, Dr. Jennie Lee Epps, scolded me for approaching the subject in that manner, but she had no idea what joy and delight it gave me.

Good conversation was one of the major entertainments in Madison. There wasn't a great deal to do; so a spontaneous conversationalist was always in demand. Charlie's cousin, Mary Baldwin, could hold my ear for long periods of time. It is rare indeed to be enthusiastic and refreshed by just listening. In fact, conversation is a lost art. Mary went to LaGrange College, where I also went, and even there she used to gather girls around her and keep them electrified for long periods of time by the richness of her tall tales. I admired her gift for talk and felt that she was the finest conversationalist I knew; this was probably because at this age I did not know too many people. The Baugh twins, May and Mable, had parents who owned a large scuppernong arbor, and they were generous about sharing its tasty grapes. Many afternoons, when the weather was especially warm, were spent under the cool arbor and by being enthralled by Mary's account of her rich and demanding life. The scuppernong has a thick, brown or purple skin that is not eaten. You squeeze the grape and discard the outside covering. It has an uncommonly good taste. I was thinking how much modern city kids miss when their time is plotted and planned just to keep them occupied. Another form of entertainment in a small town was dining out, usually in the home of a friend. Good Southern cooks are unexcelled. They are creative cooks with a light touch, rather than the heavy hand thought of as Southern cooking. They know how to make use of the many fresh garden vegetables, fruits, melons and berries that are always available. My Aunt Mable said that Uncle Bill would not come to dinner (often served at midday) unless she had seven vegetables on the table.

Our cook had her own method and order for serving. Unless we were expecting guests, we started the meal with soup, then numerous vegetables with hot cornbread. The main course was meat, hot biscuits, potatoes (often yams) followed by salad and dessert. The evening meal was called supper and was such things as oyster stew or brains and eggs or smoked salmon and salads. My mother's greatest delight was to have a large number of people at her table for every meal; therefore, it was rare to have a meal alone with my parents. My favorite vegetables were tender young turnip greens cooked with a ham hock, small white turnips, homemade cucumber pickle served with thin brown cornmeal pancakes cooked in a black frying skillet on top of the stove. I also liked hot, sweet potato biscuits that were usually too thin to cut open. Ambrosia was a special holiday dessert. In our house it was made from fresh oranges, pineapple, a coconut that my father peeled and grated, and a few toasted pecans. Three or four large pecan trees grew in our yard, so we tended to use them generously in cooking.

6

On one corner of our house was a large fig tree and on the opposite corner a pomegranate tree. Rest assured there were recipes that incorporated both. A delicious and beautiful green salad for autumn is one that has bright red pomegranate seeds sprinkled over it. During the hot summer days people of all ages regularly appeared at our house with blackberries to sell. My mother used them for pies and dessert.

Peaches were prevalent. They were one of our few commercial endeavors. On the outskirts of town were large peach orchards. After I moved to New York my mother sent me a crate of peaches each summer. She had a ritual of going herself to the packing shed to select each peach. She inevitably chose those that were soft and ripe, so when Railway Express delivered them they were crushed! They were always instructed to take the package directly to the garbage pail. I didn't have the heart to tell her. I felt she enjoyed the ritual too much to spoil it for her. She also sent six quarts of fig preserves, but they were too sweet for my taste.

These carefree days were filled with energy and motion. I was gung-ho for each new adventure, apathy was an unknown word.

One day I went on a safari to Africa to see the animals, or I rescued the children of China. I believe that at this age I had aspirations to become a missionary, but even then there was an impulsive streak in my character. My father had arranged with the town stable for me to have a horse to ride on occasion. Invariably, I picked the restless stallion who needed exercise. I rode the horse for almost three miles to the old town college, but when I turned him to head home, he would take off like a flash of lightning until we were inside his stall. He would come to an abrupt halt so I would slide forward over his head and land on my backside.

Twilight was a soothing and splendid time of the day. I sat in an informal garden and reflected on the adventures that had preceded. This unrestricted garden no doubt had an influence on the gardens in my Roxbury home. They are freeform and filled with wild flowers collected along the countryside, and beautiful weeds that come to make their home among the blooms. I like the skunk cabbage, the high rush grass, Queen Anne's Lace, and the goldenrods. To me, they add character and substance. In the beginning I carefully planted and transplanted when the flowers were in bloom so that the look of the garden would be aesthetically appealing, but soon a large rain would flood away the most delicate plants. One spring when I was in Spain the rain destroyed the entire length of the garden. The pool was frozen over with a thick ice so the large amounts of water had no place to go. It saddened me, so I decided to give the garden its head and let it make its own way. Oddly enough it has done well for itself. It grew like topsy and proved to be a satisfying spot with six shades of red phlox, sedums, four colors of bee balm; bright red is my favorite. The bee balm spreads easily, but it is a favorite winter food for water animals such as the muskrat. It is not uncommon to see a muskrat swim across the pond with an entire plant in his mouth. I like painted daisies, four shades of day lilies and numerous others: Astilbe, poppies, candy tufts, Jacob's ladder, Russian iris, fox gloves, peonies, ferns, hosta, yucca, three shades of Connecticut asters, lupins, red clover and almost anything appealing I can find.

The blackberry vines invariably find their way into the flower beds so I let them stay because they delight the birds. Any plant that brings joy to the birds can't be all bad. In the midst of this, I have sprinkled sage plants of grey and white. They add dimension and contrast. A garden is such a comfort. It touches one's heart to follow the hummingbirds as they go from one bloom to another.

I once worked on a *Vogue* cover of a Roger Vivier shoe made from a rose printed fabric. Dick Rutledge was the photographer, and we decided to use the hummingbird as though he were drinking from one of the roses. It was at this time that I did a study on the life and habits of hummingbirds and found that their metabolism is so high they must continue eating if they are to survive.

We rented a stuffed hummingbird from the Museum of Natural History and after much experimentation improvised a way to vibrate the bird so it looked real. We connected a piano wire to the bird and then to a blender. When the blender was turned on the bird looked as if he were drinking from the rose. The piano wire was airbrushed out and the result was surprisingly realistic.

To me a garden must have a will of its own. Someone once said, in hopes of pleasing me, "Your garden looks like Monet's." Naturally that was a great untruth but the nicest compliment. I planted about one hundred hemlock trees on the far side of the pond and over the last thirty years they have grown to enormous heights, like great lacy cathedral steeples that reach for the sky, and in so doing, provide a soothing, patterned backdrop for the ferns, pool, and garden. They delight me as I watch them in motion nodding and whispering one to the other in the wind, or snuggling together in the snow. Also, they stay green in the winter and look dramatic and magnetic when covered with snow. They draw me to them and invite me to stay for awhile.

A garden is such an adventure, such a satisfaction, something to enjoy and cherish. I find the changes so rewarding, so appealing, so amusing. It's active with bumble bees, butterflies, birds, chipmunks and fairies. *Every garden has fairies.* You couldn't ask for more!

Unfortunately my garden is inclined to have more greenery than blooms, but I find that I am attracted to patterns in the different shades of greens as well as to blooms. The entirety of this garden is made up of perennials that tend to spread. This eliminates the necessity for weeding and also helps hold in moisture because the plants are crowded together. They are so firmly packed that they give you a feeling of mystery after darkness when you wonder what goes on underneath their great clusters. What secrets do they keep?

One of the loveliest of green plants is lemon mint. It makes the house smell good and it is wonderful in drinks and salads. It spreads and reseeds itself. I have planted it under my bedroom window so that when the wind blows, the fragrant scent of lemon fills the room. The Roxbury soil is not good for roses, at least mine isn't, but it is custom made for hydrangeas. I dry the hydrangeas and I also dry the sage. This is not the herb for cooking; it is a plant the Indians used for medicinal purposes.

My Roxbury property is on five levels and the problem existed of what to do with the banks. I planted myrtle, a rewarding ground cover that has charming blue blooms and stays green all through the winter. It spreads easily and is hearty.

Oh, the joy of one's garden, especially with the sound of the waterfalls as background music. Each spring it reappears with new hope, new rewards, even new faces. My dog Dugan seems always happy, smiling and loving, and he makes me happy. He is so captivating, so proud, such a generous giver — he could fill an entire book. So could a garden.

It would be remiss to speak of the garden without giving some space to the numerous birds that inhabit it and the yard. Gay Talese wrote an article some time ago called "Vogueland." He seemed to be searching for some strangeness in the editors he interviewed. He said that the Baron de Geinsberg slept in a coffin; he did in a movie. And Kay Hays was a bird watcher. I am. To me that was a compliment. For a large number of years I kept a notebook in one of my bathroom windows that overlooks the bird feeder. I recorded the birds that came first in the spring, how long they stayed, and the date when they left. This year, when I had my thirty-fifth anniversary at *Vogue* they wondered what I wanted for a gift. Even though I have several, I wanted a pair of the best binoculars made so I could capture the birds in flight and enjoy the sailboats in the great salt lake in Block Island.

The mourning doves, always in pairs, have an iridescent color to their greyness and they seem so loving and affectionate. Some snowy days I can count about fourteen to twenty in one large rock maple tree. I understand that both the male and the female hatch the eggs. The male may sit on the eggs for as long as eight hours each day.

Each time I see a pair of cardinals, I am filled with delight. They are so colorful, and I think they bring good luck.

The red-winged black bird is equally beautiful and colorful. A nuthatch and a downy woodpecker are fun to watch because they are upside down birds that go up the tree backwards. A gold-finch, a chickadee and a tufted titmouse with his distinctive crest are plentiful, but I'm attracted to the slate-colored junco sparrows and wrens. They seem so friendly and so constant. I think of them as the common bird.

When the countryside is covered with a strong, silent freeze and the waterfalls and streams are hushed almost as though they were holding their breath, the birds are neither silent nor still. They act as infallible weather forecasters. Weathermen are seldom sure of themselves and seldom right when they are sure. The birds know about the weather and they tell by their excited behavior around the feeders. Even when nervously anticipating snow or a storm, they still maintain a strict protocol as to who should feed first. It is interesting to see that the beautiful cardinals are high-ranking ground feeders and that the male and female usually feed together.

A large, round raccoon, with rings on his tail and a dark mask around his eyes all fat and groomed for his partial winter hibernation, took my suet basket, wire hanger and all, to his cold-weather family retreat. It pleased me to know that he and his family would have the suet for their holiday feast. I watched through my upstairs window, filled with admiration at the intelligent way he figured out how to free the hanger from the tree, and was amazed at how well he used his fingers.

The opossum has neither the skill nor the sense of the raccoon. If you surprise him, when he is at the feeder, he just sits on a limb and covers his eyes. He thinks that you can't see him because he can't see you. Who knows, it just may be his sense of humor that causes him to cover his face.

There is a particular medium small bird that looks like a brown thrush, but isn't nearly so distinguished, who builds her nest in the garden each year. I observe her when I go for a swim in the pond, and so I am aware of the time she sits on her eggs. One July Sunday morning a friend and I were having breakfast on the terrace when the darling bird landed almost at my feet, chattering then flying back and forth to her nest. I spoke to her, as I do to all creatures. They seem to understand me, and I them. I said that she was so happy as though she were announcing the birth of her babies. It seemed too soon according to my timing, but when she continued her visits, I followed her and, sure enough, four small mouths were open waiting to be fed. Their eyes were still closed so it was a new birth, one that I enjoyed sharing with the proud new mother.

It is 3:45 a.m., I am in my Beekman Place apartment in New York. I can't seem to sleep. Why not get dressed and drive to the country? As I lay sleepless I reminisced on how I found my Maisonette on Beekman Place. At this time I had been an editor at

11

Vogue for three years and it seemed a proper time to locate a larger apartment. I already decided that the place I most wanted to live was Beekman Place. Not only is it a beautiful, private, two-block street, east of First Avenue between Mitchell Place and 51st Street, but it is residential, quiet and reminds me of a small town.

Each Saturday evening, I bought the *N.Y. Times* and searched the apartment ads. There wasn't one chance in a thousand that I would get what I wanted, but I didn't know or believe that. This particular Saturday I found an ad for a five-room apartment for rent on Beekman Place. Immediately I phoned but no answer. So sure that the apartment was meant for me, I sent a telegram that said, "*Vogue* editor very interested. Please call any hour." Two days passed and no call, but still I would not let go of my high hopes. Early on the third day, I received a call from the present tenant explaining that he had rented the apartment immediately and because he had so many calls, he went out. The man who rented the apartment, but had not taken possession, was transferred to California and the only record he had kept was my telegram — so I got the apartment. It needed some help but I was glad to invest the time and money in making two rooms into one large bedroom/sitting room. I removed several walls and met with many difficulties. One Sunday, I went over to see what had been accomplished and found four pipes and a house phone standing in the middle of my bedroom. Also the floors of the two rooms were several inches different in height. I was heartbroken, but if there is a will, and I had the will, so gradually everything fell into place. I have lived here happily, now for over thirty years. In the meanwhile it has gone co-op and I gladly bought my dream apartment.

On the dead of the moon and the night of a full moon, I seem to be too stimulated to sleep. It would be interesting to know how many people these two moon nights affect. When I was in the Danbury Hospital during April, I rang for the nurse in the wee hours and she was delayed in coming. When she appeared she explained that the hospital was pulsating with activity and that it usually is on the night of a full moon. Even old people who had no idea that it was a full moon were restless and demanding. I wish I knew if it is imagination or if the moon really has power over our lives.

12

When the weather is warm and beautiful, I spend as much time as I can out-of-doors. The air is pure, clean, crisp. Autumn had come. Can winter be far behind? Last week when I arrived in Roxbury I was greeted by an oversized pile of wood that had been delivered during the week. It looked so friendly, secure, inviting. The fire, the books, the white wine go hand in hand. There is a little sampler framed over one of my oversized fireplaces that says:

"Old wood to burn,
Old wine to drink,
Old friends to trust,
Old books to read."

We will have a hard winter this year; at least the animals seem to say so. Several weeks ago the squirrels were trying, during the day, to get into the large outside trash basket where I store birdseed. The birds seem busier than usual and even the snakes sleep on the grass, fat and filled, for their winter hibernation.

Today I left New York at 5:30 a.m. so I could see the sun rise. This is an exhilarating experience for a night person like me, especially at a time of the year when the fall leaves are just turning. The colors are almost too strong when the leaves are at their height, but that is a good ten days away. The combination of part light, part color, part grey is thrilling.

Conversation, one way, is not unusual for me. I talk to the morning, the greenery. On the two-hour trip up I had a lengthy chat with Shamus about the time the sun would rise. It became almost light at 6:30 but the first glimpse I had of the sun was at ten to seven. It partly showed over the hemlocks for less than a minute then slipped away into the fog. The last twenty miles were mysterious. When we reached Exit 14 on Route 84, I could hardly recognize the landscape.

It is 7:00 a.m. The children stand chilled and shadowy in the mist as they wait for their school bus. It is nostalgic to see them, first two, then four, then one. Many times when I drive at night I wonder who lives in these houses, and what they do and feel.

Each time I visit the Hurlbuts I feel warm and caressed by their presence. They live on a farm that is in the center of the village. The farm has been in their family for many years. In 1776, eighteen

13

Hurlbuts were landowners in what is now Roxbury. Their ancestors purchased the land from the Indians, and legend has it that the original deed was written on tree bark.

Lewis and Ethel are beautiful people. They have eight children. All eight were born and raised on the farm. It is a luxury to get eggs, raspberries, cauliflower, plums, peaches, melon, squash and corn from an atmospheric family farm. Ethel is lovely looking, somewhat delicate, shy, with a quick smile and seemingly unperturbed by stress, motherhood or hard winters. The fruit and vegetable stand is manned by her in the afternoon only; however, it is always open. A fruit jar left inside is used to hold the money. Customers take away their Hurlbut treasures and leave behind a price that is far too modest. As the children grow up they run the vegetable stand and Ethel busies herself with other things.

There is a graceful weeping willow tree directly overlooking my lower dam. I planted it years ago. A number of weeks ago I cut several medium-sized branches, removed their leaves, and placed them in water, making sure the stems were in both water and dirt. This morning I took them from their watery nest. Each one had lovely white hairy roots. These cuttings will find a happy home with someone for whom I especially care. This is a token of love from my house to theirs.

One Christmas, Susan Fine gave me a treasured group of presents. Each one came from one of her houses, bay leaf from Co. Galway, Ireland, lobster claw crackers and oversized red checked napkins from Maine, an orange covered with cloves from Connecticut. The pomander ball, after several years, still hangs from the old pewter chandelier over the dining room table. This room was once a cooking-in-the-fireplace kitchen. It has undergone only the slightest possible changes. The mill house is "cluttered," think some people, but not me. It is a happy place that seems to envelope one. How fortunate that I bought it, or perhaps it bought me.

The first time I drove to Roxbury was to bring my first Kerry Blue to a kennel, Southdown, that is no longer in operation. The countryside reminded me of my home town in Georgia. The vegetation is different and the architecture is saltbox rather than colonial, but even so I loved it and I bought the house twelve minutes after we met. This was at five p.m. on Sunday. The closing was Tuesday, and I moved in with two beds and one chair.

Never was there such a glorious day as Saturday. The temperature was in the late 30's when my house guest and I sat down to an early breakfast. By eleven the crisp pure breezy morning was warm enough to sit on the terrace. A friend and Taffy (her spirited Welsh terrier) drove from Kent to spend the day with us. We went out to lunch and then did some marketing. I found myself singing as we walked out of Gristede's at Heritage Village. My new car hadn't started easily (something about the automatic choke), and I had arisen with a wicked hangover but the beauty of the day outweighed such trivia.

I mentioned Taffy briefly, but any dog with her fire, spirit and cunning deserves a better introduction. She is my favorite dog, after Shamus. Even allowing for the highly-strung nature of the terrier, she must be a Gemini. Her personality is either strong and wicked, or sweet and loving. I have owned three Kerry Blue terriers (Sunday lived to age fourteen, Andy to age eight, and Shamus is now six), and Taffy has had a ferocious dislike for Andy and Shamus, the two she knew. One cold snowy winter's day she grabbed Andy by the throat and held tightly to his jugular vein until we poured cold water down her mouth. We have tried to figure out why, and the conclusion is that she is jealous of any dog that belongs to me. She loves me and knows that I adore her, so why should there be another dog to complicate the picture. I have just been informed that Taffy is really a Taurus — wouldn't you know it? That explains her tenaciousness.

Sunday is a cold, dank day and my spirits have dropped considerably. I can't help but think about Southerners as I've reread *The Lonely Hunter*, a biography of Carson McCullers by Virginia Carr. Perhaps I should confess to a few shortcomings about Southerners. They always talk about the weather, and they are passionate about everything. One day during Jessica Daves' lifetime, she, Armi Ratia, and I were lunching in the Cosmopolitan Club. A friend passed our table and inquired about Robert Parker, Miss Daves' husband. After she had been assured that Rob was well, the friend walked on to her table with the comment, "I just love Rob." Armi, a strong formidable

15

Finn, spoke, "Americans love everything — even potatoes. When a Finn says love, he means *love*." We smiled, and when Armi left the table to keep an appointment, Miss Daves said, "That woman scares me to death. I wouldn't dare disagree with her." True, most Americans have a passion for practically everything, and a tendency to overstate, but a true Southerner excels in this department. When the Southern passion concerns involvement, I find it rather stimulating, but deliver me from the ones who feign poverty while living in luxury, and talk continuously about goodness. I am suspicious of anyone who talks about his own goodness. I much prefer someone whose wickedness shows. At least they are more interesting and refreshing.

The first autumn I came to the Roxbury mill, in 1959, was filled with surprises, delights, and anxieties. After the leaves had fallen from the large maple trees, I found that on a clear day I could catch a glimpse across the water, on the mountainside, of three old worn grayed gravestones. At first I had mixed feelings about this sometimes autumn and winter view, but by the time the trees grew too tall to afford me the sight, I realized that I liked seeing the gravestones. They gave me a link with the past, to those who had lived in this lovely farming village, seen the same sights, been quieted by the sounds from the waterfalls, observed the wild mink, the raccoons and the deer — absorbed the silences through their skins.

When I was a child, possible five years of age, I lived in Covington, Georgia, a small town about thirty-five miles southeast of Atlanta. It was at this time that my grandmother died, and I was taken to the funeral by my mother and father. This, my first and last funeral, had a strong effect on me and I still remember dreaming about it for several nights. I couldn't accept the fact that my warm, gentle, loving grandmother was lifeless in a casket, and that she was then placed in the cold earth and left there alone. I tried to stay with her, but my parents forcefully pulled me away and took me home. Several days passed and my thoughts were still with my grandmother, so much so that I arose early one morning and walked three miles in the frosty chill to be with her. My father found me sitting beside her grave weeping. I still think of her and miss her.

16

This experience has stayed with me, and I haven't been to another funeral, including that of my mother and father, not because I didn't love them dearly, but because I could not let them go in that manner. They understood my feelings for we talked about it long before either one died, but I'm not sure that a number of others close to them understood my desperation about funerals and those I love. Perhaps it is natural, all things considered, that I had misgivings about the ancient cemetery that rested near my back road, the quietest neighbor I could have chosen. The first action I took was to visit the graveyard and accept it for what is was — a beautifully grassed hilltop that looked protectively down on my valley. This day of my visit had a strange change-of-season kind of atmosphere; the wind was strong and possessive as it sometimes is on a day in March; the temperature was nearly fifty degrees; and yet periodically a handful of snow would find its way down to the warming earth. My sweet Kerry Blue Shamus adored such a day. It was tailor made for his restless terrier temperament. He ran with the wind, very like a young colt kicking up his heels and bobbing his head as he sped from the lower gates back to the house. Watching him make this run always gave me great pleasure.

It was almost too windy to make the trip, but I felt the visit could wait no longer. The time had come for me to face the harmless dust that rested behind the moss-covered dry stone walls and the aged hemlocks no further from my property than the width of a small town road, appropriately named Hemlock Road. My living room was warm and pleasing. An active fire burned in the early cooking fireplace, and the full-toned high fidelity sounds from my music room filled the house. Both were inviting me to stay inside, to rest and refuel myself with the enjoyment of my paintings and the delicate tingles that floated in when the wind played on the Soleri bells that hung from the maple trees in the yard. It was all tempting and appealing, but inside my being I knew that this was the day to make my short, hard, curious pilgrimage.

The cemetery had an unexpected charm about it, and even some humor. There were names like Trowbridge, Squire, Norton, Hazelton, Hurlbut, Smith and next to a number of stones were markings that indicated who had served in the Revolutionary War. Major Hurlbut died in 1813 at the age of forty-five; Richard Smith in 1805, at the age of thirty-six.

One stone told of a family history of Thomas Weller, 1680-1751, and his wife Elizabath, 1690-1770, each of their eight children: Rose, 1714; Elizabath, 1716; Mary, 1718; Samuel, 1722; Abigail, 1727; Daniel, 1729; Zaccheus, 1731, and amazingly, their youngest child named Experience, 1736. As I walked through the uneven rows of weathered, crumbling, leaning headstones, many of which had long since surrendered their names and data to the passing years, I felt a strange magnetic fascination for the surroundings and for those who slept there and I longed to know more about the residents and their relationship to the village.

Roxbury had a charming librarian named John Humphry who lived in the town all of his life; so I phoned him for information. He told me that this particular cemetery was called the Weller Cemetery. It must surely be named for the family with Elizabath (spelled bath) and the eighth child delightfully named Experience.

It seems fitting to discuss Jason, my new admirer, at this time, for he belongs to the cemetery. Jason is a large, dramatic, and imposing jet-black crow who seems to have made his nest in the cemetery. At least he flies to and from that direction.

Last weekend was the long Decoration Day welcome to summer. Thus far this year, we have not been favored by many sunny spring days and suddenly, as if on cue, summer arrived, hot and inviting. Usually by this time I am well on my way to a good tan in the all-together, and have made the freezing plunge into my granite bottomed pool which is fed by cold mountain streams. Guests and friends, past and present, do not take so readily to this chilling experience as I do, but I love it, am invigorated by it, am convinced that the cold water tightens my skin and helps erase the winter stress lines from my face, and builds character!

Last Saturday as I lay sunning on a cot in the backyard, behind the house, I was attracted by a beautiful black crow that was perched on the limb of a catawba tree nearby. As I inhaled the fragrance from the lilac trees and the newly cut grass, I realized that he too was filling his nostrils with the same perfume. Almost immediately we shared; we were friends. He moved with grace and dignity when I moved, always to the tree that was nearest to me. When I left the lower yard and sat on the terrace with a cool drink, he sat there proud and strong on a branch just above me. A friend came for a drink, and he flew away, but when we moved inside the house I noticed from the window that he returned and sat on the wall not a foot away from where I had been sitting. His curiosity and seeming devotion have touched me and I feel that I would like to tame him, if only I had the patience to do so. He has been given the name of Jason and I plan to teach him his name. I am told that crows are intelligent and as protective as a watchdog. Perhaps my most difficult task will be, not just to tame him but rather, to have him accept Shamus and make sure that Shamus does not display a jealous temperament towards a living creature that has invaded his domain.

The old mill and its wooded acres is inhabited by numerous different kinds of wild animals. All are welcomed. The deer play in my yard as though it were their private park.

Raccoons have lived in the house two different winters. I have a Franklin stove in the studio on the top floor. One spring, my housekeeper, Peg Murray, heard a noise in the stove and found a pair of raccoons who had come in and out each day, down the chimney through the stove pipes into the stove. The female was soon to become a mother; so it was important that she be handled with loving care. A young man in the village has a special knowledge of such things. He came and put them in a large metal outside garbage can and took them to the town dump so they would have plenty of food to tide them over during their new birth.

I had a wire cover put over the chimney so next winter a family lived in the cellar. Thus far, they haven't done any harm to the house, but they can be destructive.

The second week in August an animal that I refer to as a wild mink - it looks like one - swims down the stream periodically going by land, then by water again. She has a loud call so that the two or three babies following her will not get lost. This family continues on down the stream, and then in about twenty minutes, the mother returns alone. One assumes that this is her way of sending the children out on their own. It's a bittersweet moment. I wonder if she feels proud or if she is sad to let them go. Perhaps a little of both.

I was awakened very early Saturday morning by the sniffing sounds from Shamus. He was standing with one front leg raised as a hesitant pause before he made the next step, staring into a corner at I wasn't sure what.

Past experience from country living had taught me that some small animal had inadvertently found his way into the house and into my bedroom. Perhaps he came down the chimney (there was a cover over the fireplace) or perhaps he came to the bedroom because he was lonely and he heard sounds.

Years of weekending in the country had taught me that such things do happen and more importantly, that something must be done because they seldom go away by themselves. I got out of bed and found that the small animal at the end of Shamus' stare was a grayish-green baby flying squirrel.

My house guest heard the commotion from another room and came to help. The first step seemed to get Shamus downstairs so that he wouldn't frighten the squirrel. I have tried to teach him not to hurt animals, but one can't be sure. So I did this while my guest kept an eye on the unexpected visitor.

His capture was necessary, and yet he must not be hurt, which meant that I should not try to pick him up. Also, I was told that squirrels sometimes bite. I trapped him behind the fire screen that stood against the wall, but he was too clever for that, so he escaped and ran under the bed. This made the entire procedure more difficult because of the dust ruffles. Finally, we encouraged him into my bathroom, but he made a flying jump over my shoulder when I bent down to persuade him to go into a trash basket.

After several additional attempts to get him into the basket he ran inside, and my guest brought me a large bath towel to cover the opening. We took him downstairs to the outside, and I gently turned the basket on its side to free him. He seemed neither upset nor anxious. In fact, he walked over to the bird feeder and proceeded to leisurely enjoy an early morning breakfast.

Sometime later, over orange juice, my guest noticed that he had left and wondered aloud where he might have gone. I didn't wonder for I felt sure that he had returned to his cozy nest somewhere in the walls of my old mill, and had been scolded by his mother for getting into trouble.

I wish him well. I also hope he learns to sleep in and begin his adventures at a more respectable hour.

Living in New York City is an exhilarating and demanding experience. After all these years, it would be difficult for me to be happy in any other city. Manhattan belongs to me, and I to it. We fit together temperamentally and emotionally. We challenge each other; however, New York as an all-time diet is too much. It tends to cause burnout and exhaustion. I especially need a change of scene, a weekend pause to refresh myself.

Come Friday, I shift gears and head for the country. I go first to Harry, Stanley and Allen of Green Valley Foods, who have a freshly cooked chicken and eggs waiting for me, the Koreans for the finest fruits and vegetables, the Artichoke for bread and salads. For years, Shamus sat in the car on the seat beside me. This trip is about two hours. When we reached the turnoff from highway 684 to 84 he reminded me by patting my leg. When we came to exit 14 he told me. I believed that he knew because we had made the trip together so many times, but now in less than four months Dugan does the same. I can't imagine how they know even when it's dark.

Soon after arriving, almost without thinking, I find that I have adjusted my pace to the pace of the country. I explore, admire, inquire and inhale the magic that kindles the imagination, feeds the spirit, cleanses the pores of my skin.

Nature can be harmonious or wild and wooly, arousing or exhilarating, demanding, fascinating and sometimes fierce and destructive, but seldom boring. As I sit on the terrace I admire the glistening mountain streams inhabited by the huge granite stones, like sculptures washed and molded by the waterfalls, protecting the secrets hidden underneath. These massive stone tablets offer hiding places for the rainbow trout, crayfish, frogs, and an occasional snapping turtle. The virgin forest that covers the largest part of my property is friendly and comforting, tall, regal and strong. We humans seem fragile by comparison. There's nothing weak or subtle about a three hundred year old tree. It has a magnificence all its own.

As night closes in, I am reminded of a brief love affair I had with a college man from the University of Georgia, when I was in high school. He was the apple of my eye. He had a seamless beauty. I had high hopes of sharing an exciting summer together. One night he brought me the sheet music of "Deep Purple." I used to play it over and over, much to the distress of my mother. I would think how romantic the twilight was. "When the deep purple falls over the sleepy garden walls and the stars begin to flicker in the sky."

One day, before our evening date, I went to the local hairdresser to get my hair done. Something happened and she gave me such a short cut that my ears showed. I hated it and cried thinking how unattractive I looked. I was apparently right, because that night the all-consuming, sophisticated, college man and I broke up. To this day, I still think of him when I hear "Deep Purple."

> "In the midst of a memory,
> You wander back to me
> Here in my deep purple dreams."

Four Editors-In-Chief
of
Vogue
and
Alexander Liberman

There have been four editors-in-chief of *Vogue*: Edna Woolman Chase, Jessica Daves, Diana Vreeland and presently Grace Mirabella. Edna Woolman Chase came to *Vogue* in 1895, at the age of eighteen. This was her first, and as it turned out, her only job. In 1914 she became editor and remained for thirty-eight years. When I came to *Vogue* in 1951 Mrs. Chase was still working, but not everyday. She resigned after fifty-six years — up until the beginning of 1952, from her active editor-in-chief position to become chairman of the editorial board.

Mrs. Chase was a small, mild-looking woman who packed a wallop. She spoke of herself in her early days as being a little midget. Born in Asbury Park, N.J., she was raised by her grandparents in a sober, loving, but severe Quaker family. Fashion was alien to her. She began her career at *Vogue* in the circulation department, admitted that she became the editor by a process of osmosis, and her name first appeared on the masthead as editor in 1914.

She readily admitted that in addition to the sewing machine in 1846, it was the influx of immigrants into America who were responsible for building the garment industry. German clothing dealers came in 1850, Italian needle workers in 1900 and then those from Eastern and Central Europe: Romania, Austria, Poland, and Russia. They worked eighty-four hours a week for little more than ten dollars.

Edna was much taken with the work of Edward Steichen, who started working for *Vanity Fair* in 1923 and continued his association with Conde Nast for fifteen years. Steichen said that the difference between a good photograph and a bad one was the quality of "aliveness." His sister married Carl Sandburg and they were close friends. Edna said in her book:

> "In some respects he was a difficult character to cope with on a magazine: fiercely independent, temperamental as an old-school opera star, and holding, Conde and I occasionally felt, an inflated idea of the value of a fashion sitting."

Late in Steichen's life he married a very young woman named Joanna. It just happened that she took an apartment in the same building on Beekman Place where I lived, but I did not know her. One evening I was invited to a preview showing of a Gordon Parks film. Standing with him at the door was an attractive young lady. Gordon introduced me to Joanna Steichen, I smiled and told her how much I admired her father's work.

When I came to *Vogue* in 1951, Mrs. Chase was not in the office on a daily basis and even though her presence was felt, it was Jessica Daves who carried the heavy load that goes with running a magazine. The editors side-stepped here and there in order to make sure that Mrs. Chase did not give us instructions that differed from those given by Miss Daves.

I. Miller had a luncheon at the Waldorf and they especially wanted Mrs. Chase to come. I'm not sure of the date, but she was already ill but not entirely inactive. I took a cab and called for her at her East 57th Street apartment. She carried something under her arm that I could not distinguish. I offered to take it but, thank God, I didn't insist. It turned out to be some type of heating pad she carried to relieve her pain. We walked down the steps at the Waldorf to the luncheon room. Someone made the mistake of taking her small under-arm package. She screamed loudly, and it was then that I realized how uncomfortable she must be.

During the luncheon she was charming and even drank three martinis. Everyone was pleased that she had come, and I feel it did her good. When I took her home we sat in the cab in front of her apartment talking for twenty or thirty minutes.

She wanted me to understand what had happened between her and the shoe industry. Naturally I knew the story, but I listened intently. Mrs. Chase had made a statement in *Vogue* to the effect that she did not consider open-toed shoes smart or fashionable. She was speaking of the open-toed pump. Her statement was misunderstood and shoe sales, both wholesale and retail, plunged downward. Her comment had seemed a small thing, and it wasn't without merit. However, it got out of control, and she spent years trying to make it up to the industry.

I. Miller, then owned and operated by the Miller family, had a strong and important influence upon shoe fashions. When Mrs. Chase's statement appeared, their stock dropped six points, and the sales on all open-toed sandals in the stores dropped to nothing. The entire incident was a misunderstanding and Mrs. Chase always regretted that it had happened. Her last effort to make this appearance at an I. Miller showing, when she was well into her eighties and ill, seemed dear and touching to me. It showed her depth of concern, how much she cared, her great sense of fairness and her deep desire to right a wrong she had inadvertently created.

I wanted to, and tried to, relieve her mind of this nagging about a thing long past and so small by comparison to all the big and excellent things she had brought to the fashion world. The part she played in the creation and growth of Seventh Avenue is tremendous. She started the fashion show as it is known today.

I would like to quote from *Always in Vogue*, a book written by Mrs. Chase and her delightful daughter, Ilka.

> "Amid the steel and cannon, the bloodshed and the slaughter, the furbelows of the dressmaking business may seem frivolous but it must be remembered that in France the couture is both an art and a vital industry in which the government has taken a lively interest. The French dressmakers were caught at the very moment of showing their Fall collections, involving thousands of people and millions of francs."

In late August John Wanamaker placed an announcement in the New York papers, written by their buyer Mr. Hoffman, the story of many Americans concerned with fashion who found themselves in Paris in the early days of the First World War, desperately trying to get out with models for the American trade. I quote it in part:

> "What shall I do?" I said to myself, "Have I come three thousand miles for nothing? Shall America have no Paris fashions this autumn? We shall see—!" I left the waiting crowds in front of the Embassy clamoring for passports. I turned

away and started to make the rounds of the couturiers. Callot was not ready. Cheruit promised an exposition the thirteenth. "Women must have clothes, war or no war, " said Madame Cheruit, "and those who make them must have a way to earn their living. We shall keep open and make what we can." I went to the beautiful atelier of Paul Poiret. He was in the blue and scarlet uniform of the French infantry surrounded by a crowd of weeping women, his devoted helpers. "I am going to join my regiment," he said calmly, "an artist is nothing when a soldier is wanted. France needs men today, not artists." "But have you nothing ready? No models that I may show to America?" "No, the atelier is closed. It shall remain closed with nothing touched until I return, if I do return." I passed out silently. At the famous Rue de la Paix house of Worth. I was greeted by Jean and Jacques Worth, also in uniform. They were taking a last look at one of their gowns just finished. At Doeuillets on the Place Vendome the same scene was repeated. Monsieur Doeuillet had joined the volunteers but a few gowns were made up and these I procured ... my greatest opportunity came when the house of Bechoff-David was forced to close. Monsieur Bechoff also had been called to arms. His entire collection was offered to me at war prices — half the usual figures. I took them all, some two hundred garments."

Because of that windfall, Wanamaker's was cheerful, but if the trade as a whole found itself at a loss without the stamp of Paris authority, the fashion press was truly up against it.

I could not know then that after the first frightening months the French couture would resume virtually normal production and that throughout the war *Vogue* would be able to publish French models as well as the lengthy dispatches on Paris life written for us by Anna Van

Campen Stewart — stories of zeppelin drifting overhead and of long periods when the museums and theaters were dark, of the rationing of sugar and the consequent shutting down of many of the famous tea shops such as Rumpelmayer's and Colombin's. The perimeter of life continued pretty much as before except that sheep grazed in the parks and the resorts of the Midi were filled with convalescent soldiers. In a country where heavy mourning had long been a tradition, it seeped, a dark tide, through the towns and countryside as the casualty lists came back from the trenches and funerals were the macabre social life of the French capital.

A pretty young woman babbling to a wounded soldier she was supposed to be diverting, wondered aloud what the new spring wear would be. He looked at her somberly and shifted his crutches. "Mourning, madame, mourning." And so she found it. Was an event somber or gay, exciting or dreary, comical, frustrating, or tragic, the same phrase summed it up: "C'est la guerre."

These stories and all the others we learned as the months and years dragged by, but at the outbreak of the war business in the fashion world was abruptly halted, and how to fill the pages of *Vogue* became my personal problem.

Riding on top of a Fifth Avenue bus one early autumn day, racking my brains for a solution, in a flashback of memory I recalled the doll shows that *Vogue* had given in 1896, '97, '98. Those miniature ladies had been dressed by New York houses. I had an idea. Jumping down from the bus, I hastened to Mr. Henri Bendel. His shop was the smartest in New York, and his clientele was a social register of fashion. Mr. Bendel had recently established himself in Fifty-seventh Street, at that time an exclusive residential district, which he was the first to invade commercially.

He had vision, taste, and courage and was greatly respected in the fashion world in both America and France. His heart was undoubtedly as sad as mine for our unfortunate friends in Paris, but he too had a business situation to meet, and I felt that my idea might temporarily solve both our problems and benefit France at the same time.

I said, "Mr. Bendel, if *Vogue* organizes an exhibition of original designs, created by the best New York houses and presented on living models, charges admission, and devoted the proceeds to a French charity, will you head the list of exhibitors?"

I knew that if Bendel consented, the other houses would fall into line. Armed with his agreement, I flew back to the office embroidering my plans as I went.

I was full of enthusiasm and blurted out my scheme to Mr. Nast, explaining that *Vogue* could render a great service to the fashion industry, that the magazine could dramatize its role of leadership, and that I was sure we could get society patronesses if we organized the show for charity.

I did not make a quick sale. My boss was not one to tackle a new idea without looking at the proposition in the round. He foresaw, and rightly, that we would have a good many hurdles to jump.

Fashion shows have become a way of life. A lady is hard put to go to lunch, or sip a cocktail in any smart hotel or store from New York to Dallas to San Francisco without having lissome young things in the most recent models swaying down a runway six inches above her nose. It is difficult to visualize that dark age when fashion shows did not exist. Yet there was such a time and there have been moments when secretly I have wondered whether I did not render dubious service to my country the day the idea popped into my mind on the bus.

Mrs. Chase was a brilliant and tenacious woman who gave sixty years of her life to the excellence of the field of fashion. As we sat together in the intimacy of a yellow cab, with the meter running, my heart went out to this small powerful woman. I never loved her more than at that moment, and I longed for the right words to say that would reassure her that the open-toe incident had long been forgotten. I am not sure I found them. That was the last time I saw her. She died a short while after that day.

I thought you might be interested in at least two less important examples of Mrs. Chase's personality. She had a little habit that seems strange today. Periodically, she would arrive at the office before the editors and check each desk. It was not unusual to find a note from her that said, "This desk is untidy, do something about it."

Manufacturers are prone to have breakfast, cocktail, or evening showings. She would ask each secretary to give her a list of the time of each showing. If there were too many showings, before or after office hours, she would write a note to the manufacturers or retailers and ask them to confine their showings to the hours between nine and five.

Mrs. Chase closed her book, *Always in Vogue*, with advice to fashion students:

"Give yourself time to let you own impressions crystallize. Don't be carried away by the obvious and the spectacular. Everyone sees that. It is the sophisticated eye, the trained taste, that chooses at first glance the subtly simple, the elegant, the really smart dress that will outlive a dozen tricky models. Beau Brummel, that great exponent of fashion of the nineteenth century, expressed this philosophy very well when he said, 'That which characterizes elegance is that it should not be remarked.'

"Learn to see beyond the stage that dismisses everything with one or another of our popular adjectives, divine or lousy. And in the fashion business whether or not you intend to be a designer or an artist, it will become a tremendous asset to you if you learn to draw well enough to make little rough sketches. Also, if possible, develop the ability to write. Learn to write about what you see with originality, with color, and with variety. In short, if you have the sophisticated viewpoint of a woman in the smart world, the sensitive perception of the artist, the clarity of thinking of a meticulously trained lawyer and the common sense of an experienced housewife you can be an ace at the fashion game — you will also be unique."

The one person who had the greatest influence upon my early business days is Jessica Daves, and the one who most influenced my latter days at *Vogue* is Alexander Liberman. Jessica Daves served as editor for seventeen years and before that as managing editor for ten years.

Soon after I got a divorce I went to work in the fashion department in Bamberger's Department Store in Newark. I had been working there about three years when Mary Campell, the Secretary of the Board of Conde Nast and Personnel Director and at that time, head of the job department at *Glamour*, asked me if I would be willing to dress a group of late teenagers the way they should look to get a job. The Dior "New Look" had come and gone, but not to these kids. They still wore their skirts below mid-calf, and nothing could persuade them to change. I dressed each one, and when they had left I had the fitting lady take the hems up seven inches so if the girl appeared in the show she had to wear the shortened length. The clothes, well-labeled, were sent to the seminar location, and I hoped for the best.

Mary Campbell phoned me sometime later and suggested I come over for lunch. My job at Bamberger's required that I spend two or more days in New York in the market; so I agreed. After lunch Mary asked if I would like to work for one of the Conde Nast magazines. I was tired of commuting from New York to Newark everyday, but I wasn't interested in being tied to a desk. She explained that wasn't necessary and asked me which magazine I preferred. It seemed if I were going to be in publishing, I might as well start at the top, and my experience was better for *Vogue*, so I chose it.

She had me speak with Cathleen Casey, then Mildred Gilbert, and said she would phone Jessica Daves, who was at home ill. Miss Daves came in that afternoon and talked with me. She asked me where I went to college. I said it was a small woman's college in Georgia, LaGrange College. I doubted that she had heard of it. She quickly explained that she knew it well and that she was a Georgia girl from Cartersville. Her town was not far from Madison, my home town. We

30

talked for an hour and she offered me a job as Accessory and Shoe Editor in the Merchandising Department of *Vogue*. In order for the change to be worthwhile to me, financially, I felt I should come in as a full editor. She agreed, and I started to work three weeks later on February 26, 1951. Fate has taken care of me through the years. There is no way I could have survived working up through the ranks. I do not have the patience or the temperament. In less than six months Franchesca Kilpatrick resigned as Fashion Editor for shoes, and Miss Daves offered me both jobs as Fashion and Merchandising Editor for shoes. She took me for a cab ride through Central Park and explained that Mr. Nast had felt a specialized market like shoes should be handled by one person. I was doing well in the merchandising department and was not anxious to change so quickly to something I didn't know. She spoke just the right words, and I knew that I wanted to work more closely with this fantastically brilliant woman. I never regretted my decision. She was a hard task master, but I was lucky to be working with her. She taught me discipline. She made me believe that my ideas were as good as those of anyone else. She told me I could do anything I wanted to and she made me believe it. She caused me to exceed myself. If I had to decide what I thought she did best, I would say that she had a way with people.

Jessica Daves was neither a dramatic nor a beautiful woman. I knew her well from 1951 until her death. During these years she was overweight, as am I, not too tall, but despite this she had a distinguished manner. She adored real jewelry and Tatiana hats. Her dress was always fashionable but she was not impressive looking. Once she started speaking, everything changed. I was visiting Polly Clapp in Martha's Vineyard when Miss Daves' husband, Rob, died. I drove to New York to get her. We came to the country where she stayed three or four days.

Diana Vreeland was not kind to Miss Daves. When she came to *Vogue* she took over with a vengeance. She seemed to believe that *Vogue* was nothing before her time. Miss Daves had grown tired, so she resigned some months earlier than she had previously planned. I loved her and I believe she loved me. Before the announcement of her retirement, she took me to lunch, again at her beloved Cosmopolitan Club, to tell me of her plans. At this very personal meeting she asked me not to leave *Vogue* just because she was retiring, so I stayed.

Miss Daves had been a mother figure to me since the death of my own mother a few years before. I am happy to say that we remained close after her retirement. My mother was ill from April until November. I went to Georgia every weekend to be with her in the Emory University Hospital. This meant that I lost two nights' sleep, Friday and Sunday. My job was suffering, and I was thinking about quitting but had not mentioned it. My paycheck suddenly had a big increase and I asked Miss Daves about it. She said, "Just a little vote of confidence." This was typical of her kind of woman.

She and Rob came to Roxbury for Rob's eightieth birthday. I painted my wheelbarrow bright red, then painted birds and flowers on the inside so that I might wheel it to the terrace where we ate. I had colorful balloons tied to the sides. Rob loved the sculpture I had bought for him from Don Case but hated the balloons and said so.

A young boy from Bridgewater named Don Case came to me as a grass-cutter. He longed to be an artist, and I encouraged him to pursue this ambition. He went to college, driving his little MG to and from everyday, even in the winter, without windows because they had been stolen. After college he went to California to art school and while there became interested in sculpture. He brought me his winning piece called Madonna and Child. It is made of lead drippings; it is strange, appealing and sensitive. I gave it a home in my studio, and it still stands there.

One summer while Don was home from art school he asked if I would give him his first commission. I was happy to do so, but felt that he wasn't yet too accomplished, so I asked him for a stone fish for my pool. He took the stone from one of my waterfalls, and chiseled out a graceful fish. The piece was very heavy, so Don and his brother took it through the water and placed it on a large stone across the pool. It rested there until one September in 1975 when a fierce flood unseated it.

Some months after the gift of a Case sculpture to Rob, Miss Daves asked to meet Don. He went to New York to see her. She gave him a commission to do a penguin for their Park Avenue apartment. He did and they liked it.

Both Rob and Jessica Daves (her married name was Mrs. Robert Allerton Parker, but I always called her Miss Daves) had a way of calling a spade a spade. I remember going into her office to discuss an idea with her. She was very exacting and precise. I had told her about half of my creative plan when I said I wasn't sure if I was using the precise words, but she would get the meaning. She quickly replied, "When you have the proper words, come back, and we will continue the discussion."

Before they left the country, the day of Rob's birthday, I showed her my purple clematis that was blooming on the side doorway to the mill. She corrected me by saying, "In the first place, it's cle'matis, not clem'atis, and why should you show me one little bloom when you have the yard filled with blooms?"

I was proud of my gardens that year. Fortunately Rob's birthday came at a time when the garden was at its peak. The huge lacy varieties of ferns across the pool serve as a perfect backdrop for my perennial blooms. The night before the party I went to bed feeling proud and pleased that each plant had given its all for the occasion. I arose early the next morning to check all the last minute details for the dinner. As is my custom upon arising, I looked out my bedroom windows to admire the garden. At first I couldn't believe what I saw or understand how it happened. Then I saw a darling (how can I say *darling*) muskrat gaily swimming across the large fresh water pool to his hole. He carried a stalk of Queen Anne's Lace in his mouth. During the night he had taken large chunks of phlox. I was left with six or eight bare spaces. All my ambitious design planning had been for nothing. I didn't take it lightly, but at least I knew that one muskrat family had supplies for the winter.

Miss Daves was a hard task-master who expected all her staff to be in their offices by nine o'clock. If she sent for you at nine-ten when you were having coffee, under no condition was anyone permitted to take a coffee cup to her office. When one did so they were politely asked to leave.

Also, in editorial meetings you were allowed to speak as long as what you were saying was of importance. When it ceased to become so she interrupted and went on to more relevant matters.

One of the disarming qualities she possessed was her politeness. She always thanked someone when she had done them a favor. Once when I was on a business trip to St. Louis with one of our advertising men from the Chicago office, we had a little problem. He drank too much, which was not unusual for him, but this time we were at dinner with his largest account. Since this had happened before, and because I was too young and inexperienced to know how to handle the situation, I chose to excuse myself and go back to my hotel. Of the several things I might have done, this was perhaps the worse. The next morning he led me to believe that he could cause me trouble for leaving the table. That showed how little he knew about me. I always told when I had made an obvious blunder. When I returned to New York, I went to Miss Daves, told her what I had done and before I could apologize, she interrupted me with, "Good for you," her typical way to reassure the editors that she was behind them.

Once I asked her how she had the courage to send her staff out to handle speeches and unexpected situations on their own, and she replied that unless she did, the magazine would be limited to her mind, her capabilities, and she had faith in her people.

I remember her saying, "When you do something for someone you must go all the way; make them happy or don't bother." It is not unusual for the magazine to photograph striking pictures for manufacturers and for the secretaries to annoy them so much trying to get the necessary data, such as price, description, retail stores (which isn't easy), and in the process anger the manufacturers so much that they wish it never happened.

Margaret Case, *Vogue*'s society editor for many years, had been on Onassis' yacht with Elsa Maxwell and other celebrities. Weird and unspeakable happenings took place on trips such as this, so we were all ears when Margaret agreed to share the trip with us. She was both clever and amusing and had a bit of the devil in her, so we waited for her gossip. Part of the trip required that she take pictures to appear in a future issue of the magazine.

Meg, as she was called by Miss Daves (they were about the same age), had taken time and effort to put everything in writing. She had a dramatic leaning and we were her audience. Everyone was primed for the behind-the-scenes comments. Margaret spent about ten minutes telling how difficult a photographic sitting is, something we knew and understood, and how hard she had worked on her pleasure cruise. Miss Daves insisted that she get to the point or be seated. This outraged Margaret so much that she picked up her script and left the room. We continued with the editorial meeting, but poor Margaret had missed her shining hour before an enthusiastic captive audience.

Margaret was also famous for buying new clothes that were sent to the office. Upon arrival she would strip to the nude and try them on immediately. I had a secretary who said, "Miss Hays, you don't pay me enough to witness that scene."

Poor dear darling Margaret, years later when she was old, ill and felt unneeded, jumped out the window of her apartment on Park Avenue and killed herself. A sad ending for what had been a spicy, amusing, talented woman.

During the latter part of her life, Miss Daves was too set in her ways to change her politics, so she clung to the fact that a President of the United states could not be a crook. It was beneath her dignity to even suppose such a thing. As the Watergate scandal unfolded, she became more and more disappointed and upset. I will always feel that she died a broken woman.

It is sad even to think that it could happen to such a distinguished woman. She had been President of the Fashion Group, awarded the French Legion of Honor, the Italian Order of Merit, served as member of the Woman's Board of the New York Public Library and the Board of Directors of the MacDowell Colony.

I would like to share two quotes from *The World of Vogue*, first from I.S.V. Patcevitch, the publisher during Miss Daves' time, and the latter from her. This book was compiled by Jessica Daves and Alexander Liberman after her retirement. Her other two books are *Entertainment in Vogue* and *Ready Made Miracle*.

"The making of a magazine is, I dare say, quite different from manufacturing almost anything else. Our product seems at first glance, so frail, so ephemeral. It cannot be eaten or worn, or used as a building material, or driven along a highway. A magazine in its physical form — even such as *Vogue* — is, before all, simply a number of sheets of paper imprinted with illustration and text, neatly stapled together and collected beneath an eye-catching cover. It appears on and disappears from the newsstands with dreamlike rapidity. Unless carefully stored or preserved in a binding, it is perishable. With heavy or prolonged use and handling, it disintegrates.

"Yet, each issue of *Vogue*, this fragile and transitory product, performs a certain historical function. It holds a mirror up to its time; a small mirror, perhaps, but a singularly clear, brilliant, and revealing one."

I.S.V. Patcevitch

The second quote from the same book is from Jessica Daves:

"From generation to generation, the race continues to be moved by hunger, love, and fear; to seek amusement; to feel envy, desire, curiosity, and an avid interest in the new. In its pages, *Vogue* has as a matter of course reported the exterior changes; but the current of news has been only one of *Vogue*'s reasons for being. There has been, more deeply, the hope to cherish the sense of beauty, to feed the mind, to stir the imagination. And governing all has been a high regard for the best — the best of its kind, whatever the kind.

"The pages were asked not only to amuse, to stimulate, to please, to bring the news, but to present a level of judgement of quality in people, places, manners, milieu. Playwrights, laugh makers, ballerinas, pianists, painters; leading ladies and prima donnas; written to prick the mind, ideas to fire the pulse — all these have been weighed on the scale of quality.

"*Vogue* has sometimes been called a civilizing force. If that is true, perhaps it is because a civilization, to endure, needs voices to sing its praise. 'They had not poet and they died,' is Gogarty's epitaph for lost treasures of the unrecorded past. A part of civilization is a regard for the gifted, an admiration of beauty, an understanding of the arts — the arts of daily living as well as the arts of painting or sculpture, writing or music or architecture. Civilization has in it, too, respect for the boldness of the frontiersmen in the sciences and in all the worlds of abstract ideas. These things *Vogue* has recorded, dramatized, applauded. Some of the best of the record is in the pages of this book."

Jessica Daves

Diana Vreeland was a difficult woman for me, and others, at least in the beginning. She had worked for many years at *Harper's Bazaar*. When Carmel Snow died, her niece Nancy White was brought from *Good Housekeeping* and placed in the top editor's job. This must have been a big disappointment to Mrs. Vreeland.

She worked with a different attitude from the two editors-in-chief who preceded her, and Grace Mirabella who followed her. It is rather hard to explain, but she seemed to have little regard for those under her, especially the secretaries and assistants. She was electric, ruthless and a bit contagious. She seldom came to the office before 2:00 p.m.; so her time there was very dear; yet, she insisted upon passing on the smaller details. We coexisted for awhile, and I found I could avoid her for weeks if I worked it just right. After at least one blow-up between us, when I quit and ran to the country, we found a way to work together.

This was a time before the entrance of numerous textured, patterned and lace hosiery. It was coming but the mills had not yet been tooled for production. Mrs. Vreeland had her way of expecting the impossible, the more difficult, the more she insisted. One Monday morning she called me in, then very roughly announced that she expected a pair of lace tights in her office by Tuesday. The fact that they did not exist meant nothing to her unreasonableness. I too am stubborn and I played a game with her. The more impossible the job, the more resolved was I to get it done. She was not a woman to inspire those around her. Instead she bullied, brow-beat and screamed. Thus far she had not yelled at me, but surely my day would come. When she chided me for not having a lace leg covering, I began searching my mind to outwit her. There was a talented woman in the hosiery industry named Helen Sisson. I had worked closely with her, and she also lived near to me in the country. I remembered that her firm had made several prototype laces in Germany, and she used them for dramatic effects in her presentation. They were not available or buyable, but they would serve for my purpose of outfoxing Mrs. Vreeland.

It was already late in the afternoon but I called Helen, who was retired from business and living in her country home, and begged her to lend me a gold lace and a black lace. She readily agreed, but how to get them to me by morning? This was before the existence of the numerous overnight delivery services such as Federal Express; so there was no way to have these tights unless I drove to the country and picked them up. This would be a four-hour roundtrip, but I was determined. Hurriedly I rushed to my apartment, fed my dog, walked him, put him in the car and away we sped for our tiring trip.

Traffic was impossible at this time of day. As usual there was construction enroute, and it poured rain. Undaunted, I kept driving, picked up my prize and landed back at my New York apartment after three a.m.

Tuesday morning I could hardly wait to spring my surprise on Mrs. Vreeland, but of course she would not be there before lunch, and then I must wait until she chose to give me an audience. When the moment finally arrived I rushed in, excited, breathless, pleased as punch and placed not one but two laces on her desk. This time I felt sure she would smile, praise me and comment on my inventiveness. Instead she rather crossly asked me why I hadn't brought in three pairs of lace pantyhose.

That did it; I was tired and weary, and she did not even ask me how I had done the impossible and secured two pairs. My usually sleeping temper awoke, and before I knew what had happened I threw the items on her desk and told her she could keep her damn job, "I quit."

Fool that I am, I left the office, went through the same dog routine as the day before, but this time I drove to the country to my mill. By the time I reached Roxbury, I had long since calmed, but I was faced with having quit my job in a fit of anger. For three days I waited for her call to bring me back, but it didn't happen. Finally I phoned Liberman in his office, but as fate would have it, Mrs. Vreeland picked up the phone and asked where I was. When I explained, she quietly said, "My dear, you must not take things so seriously." This was our first and last shouting match. After that the going was far from easy at times, but we coexisted. Had I been less stubborn there were numerous times I would have fled for good. I refused to be beat by such a difficult woman, and I was rather stimulated by the challenge she offered me.

There were problems, but Mrs. Vreeland was not without tenderness. On the day when I realized that I must put my first Kerry Blue to sleep, I was desolate and deeply immersed in my sorrow. I phoned Mrs. Vreeland and explained that I must go to the country and be among living things. She quickly said, "Go, stay one week, one month or longer. Your job will be here. Come back when you feel ready."

The longer I knew her, the better I liked her, but things were rarely smooth between Mrs. Vreeland and her staff. Couregues was at his height of fame during these years and she was anxious to help him. He made three or four important shoes each season. They were frequently copied by American shoe manufacturers. She drove me home one day, in the limousine that picked her up each evening, and told me that I must get a manufacturer to pay him for these shoes and produce them in America. This would give him money and acclaim for his designs. To find a manufacturer was not an easy job, especially since there was nothing to prevent them from copying him without cost, but I finally persuaded the Joyce Shoe Company, a division of U.S. Shoe, to go to Paris and meet with Couregues. The appointment was set, by me, by phone, with the Couregues office.

I had misgivings about the whole thing, and it so happens my concern was justified. The Joyce executive went to Paris, arrived at the appointed time and Couregues refused to see him.

Fortunately, other adventures concerning shoe manufacturers and designers have worked better. This year (1976), Calvin Klein and Geoffrey Beene are making shoes under their name for Andrew Geller, Roger Vivier and Halston for Garolini, Ralph Lauren for Arthur Edelman, Jones, N.Y. for Palizzio, and Bill Blass for Adlib. All their shoes are made in Italy except Bill Blass and Jones, N.Y. They are made in Spain.

Diana Vreeland ruled *Vogue* with a strong hand and by so doing she added an excitement to the magazine. The pictures and layouts were more daring and stimulating than before her time.

Jessica Daves had a more sensible approach to the fashion pages. Diana Vreeland threw caution to the wind. She knew change was needed and sought to bring it about. Mrs. Vreeland was good for *Vogue* at this time. She worked hard, helped many creative people, and had a large circle of friends.

Alexander Liberman was largely responsible for the improvement to the way *Vogue* looked. He had been elevated to Editorial Director of all Conde Nast magazines, American and foreign. *Vogue* became smarter and more revolutionary in its approach to fashion. He was, and is, the one person most responsible for *Vogue*'s taste level. Alex Liberman is, and has been since he first became *Vogue*'s Art director, the creative force behind *Vogue*. He is a jewel of a man.

Liberman came to American *Vogue* from Paris where he worked for French *Vogue*. His taste, his brilliance, his genius, has made the difference between other fashion magazines and *Vogue*. I could write volumes on the man and his talent. He is attractive, sophisticated, a superb dinner companion, a dedicated artist, sculptor, writer, a professional businessman who accomplishes more than can be done by one person. I would not believe it if I didn't see it happen. Working with Liberman has enriched my life. In the subtlest way he nudges you to rise above your limits. The beauty of the man is that with all these stresses and endeavors he remains charming, and seemingly undisturbed. He has depth, dimension, conviction, integrity. Working with him is a religious and creative experience. In fact a creative love affair, so to speak. I have worked closely with, and for him for thirty-six years, and he has never raised his voice or been cross to me, even under the most tedious of conditions. He and Tatiana, his wife, visit me in Roxbury, and I visit them in Warren. We are friends, and I love and adore them. Working with Alex is a rare and cherished privilege. What a nice way to feel about your boss.

One night at a dinner party at my house I said to Virginia Goegney, seated next to him, that he was my boss. He overheard me and in his own delightful way said, "Kay is the only person at *Vogue* who doesn't have a boss." I explained that he was an important artist and sculptor. He quickly said, "Kay is a true artist. She lives her art everyday."

Neither remark is true, but gallant and indicative of the beauty and grace of this man who always turns a compliment to your advantage.

Marshall Blonsky interviewed Liberman in the 1986 summer edition of *Bomb*. It was a frank and incisive discussion. From it I chose a few statements that reflect the thinking and motivations of a man whose life is divided between magazines and pure art and sculpture:

"I have always spoken of magazines being energy pills. I think there's a subliminal reality in them, and people don't even realize it. The drive and the energy for a magazine like *Vogue*...corresponds to the American tempo. The traditional tempo of fashion used to be a slow tempo. That tempo has changed. There was a speed-up of civilization, in design. A lot of it could come from juxtaposition, from rhythm, from contrast, from color sensations. There are many things that give tempo. Typography too. Type, street poster, the whole street scene has always fascinated me. Just as film is communication, photography is communication, typography is communication and for me all this comes together in a magazine. Even today, I've had front pages of the "News" when it was very dynamic or the "Post" pinned on the walls of the art department, to jolt.

"*Vogue* is a family, a group of human beings with a common purpose. I think making life more attractive and also helping women experience life more fully. The magazine reflects the development of American women's minds. But we must never forget the delight of fashion, the pleasure, the amusement, the beauty of women. One of the things I think I've helped do is focus on what really is important and good. This is one of the areas I feel happy with.

"I'm enormously interested in the deep under-lying motives of human beings. I studied philosophy, after all, even if I'm not a philosopher. I've been very preoccupied, if that's the word, with myths and the sort of deep-seated longings of humanity, and I think there are certainly eternal values to touch on, or to attempt to touch, attempt to reveal, through art.

"I think there's a hierarchy in creativity. When people speak of the art of couture, the art of photography, all the so-called arts, I then think of what I consider the real art, it puts me in my place and I can take, without disparaging it in any way, my magazine work lightly. If I have to decide how to communicate information and where possible give pleasure, I do not put my soul into that decision. It's a professional decision. With magazines there's this great relief that there are due dates. Things have to go, perfect or not perfect. You've done your best and they're gone. But the decision of should I put this metal plate or this color an inch higher or an inch lower is a torment of days, if not a permanent torment. There are sculptures that have gone, but I still wonder if I moved this or that...I consider nothing ever finished, nothing ever really perfect."

Diana Vreeland took over in 1962. Richard Avedon came from *Bazaar* to *Vogue* sometime later. Irving Penn was still active, Norman Parkinson, Gordon Parks, John Cowan, Art Kane were a few of our best photographers. Verushka was the top model, and Balenciaga, Chanel, Dior, St. Laurent, Givenchy were making beautiful clothes. Then conditions changed in the country. The small boutique came into prominence. The youth of the country set the styles with their jeans, old clothes, ethnic leanings, handmade jewelry and other things they made and the way they wore their clothes. The expensive designer had become less important, but a woman like Mrs. Vreeland, who could spend an hour on an armhole seam, could not bring herself to accept a lesser style. About this time she and *Vogue* parted company. I was sorry, in many ways, to see her go. She is now doing an outstanding job at the Metropolitan Museum of Art and she continues to have a tremendous influence upon fashion.

Balenciaga was one of Mrs. Vreeland's favorite designers, perhaps her most favorite. In 1973 she did an exhibition dedicated to the work of Balenciaga at the Costume Institute of the Metropolitan Museum of Art. Her comments about the man are expressive and beautifully written. I wanted to share them with you:

"Cristobal Balenciaga was the true son of a strong country filled with style, vibrant color, and a fine history. He remained forever a Spaniard and his inspiration came from the bullrings, the flamenco dancers, the fishermen in their boots and loose blouses, the glories of the church and the cool of the cloisters and monasteries. He took their colors, their cuts, then festooned them to his own taste and dressed the Western world for thirty years.

"All women search for their special identity. All women have sleeping qualities of luxury and mystery. Balenciaga brought the body and dress together in harmony and suddenly a woman found herself in perfect rhythm with the universe. She found herself in delectable colors and combinations and almost impossible perfection. He loved the coquetry of lace and ribbon, of floating taffeta and racy day clothes cut with such gusto and flair of tailoring as the Western world has never known.

"He was the master tailor, the master dressmaker. His voice was low and his smile was warm. He believed totally in the grace and dignity of women and made each and every one of his devoted patrons a unique and extraordinary figure."

Grace Mirabella, the present Editor-in-Chief of *Vogue*, was described by Gardner Cowles who met her at a party as, "The most charming woman I have met." Grace and I grew up together at *Vogue*. I was twenty-eight when I came to *Vogue*; Grace came a year later. During the years when she was an assistant to Mrs. Vreeland, we had our traumas, but not today, thus far.

There is a right woman for her day, and Grace is the right woman for today. Alex Liberman has been wonderful with her, and to her, and she has been a superb Editor-in-Chief. Times have changed, and no longer is there a need for a strong unbending central figure to rule the magazine. No longer does fashion, or the fashion magazine, set the pace. Today a woman makes her own decision based on her needs and her lifestyle. If she doesn't make these decisions, she should. The job of the fashion magazine is to expose her to the best, the newest, the smartest in fashion, theater, and writing and people.

Grace has a planning meeting for each issue. She calls it a creative meeting. At this time the editors discuss, with her, the subject and philosophy of the issue, usually three or more months in advance. Clothes are then brought in for a run through. This is done after extension and perpetual market coverage by the editors. Each designer's clothes are placed on an iron rack. The editor presents her own market. The best clothes are shown on models, who have been booked for the run through. This is necessary so we can see, and examine, fit, length, and any of the assets or defects.

Photographic settings are scheduled. Photographers, models, and hairdressers are booked. The clothes are accessorized with jewelry, handbags, belts, shoes, tights, and anything else they might need. An editor is always present at a photographic sitting to make sure the fashion is presented in the right manner. She is responsible for every detail, including the models' hair.

The pictures are made in color or black and white, sometimes both. Hundreds of negatives are brought to the art department. The number depends on the size of the sitting. The best selections are chosen. They are photostated and the layouts for the pages are made from the photostats. This is done so the negatives will not be handled. These layouts are okayed by Alexander Liberman, Grace, and the editor. Each item on the page is identified by the editor.

Copy is written and the pages are sent to the engravers. We see our pages several times: Layouts without copy, color or black and white prints without copy, then with copy. Color and copy corrections are made when it becomes necessary.

It seems so simple that any fool could do it. Each step is fraught with problem possibilities: Fabrics to manufacturer deliveries may be delayed, union problems, strikes may occur, or other dramas. The retailer is tremendously important. He is the one who buys the fashion for his store. His acceptance, and the size of his orders is of paramount importance. His delivery must coincide with the date the magazine is on the newsstand. Thousands of items appear in each issue.

The assistant of each editor checks the wholesale and retail price of the item, all details pertinent to its description, such as color and type of fabric or leather, and delivery dates. This is sent in writing to the credit department. They give this information to the retail publicity department when they are offered the credit that means the store's name, usually one New York store and two out-of-town stores, will appear on the page of the magazine with the fashion that is shown.

The retail salesperson is the next link in the chain. Manufacturers and designers can spend many long months, from the time they start with the fabric to the time the clothes reach the store. The retailer may have advertised it nationally in a magazine, on television, or in a newspaper. He may have it on display in the windows or in the department where it is sold.

A salesperson, her attitude, her understanding of fashion, can make or break its chance of success.

Today an editor must not only know, but have an influence upon, her markets. Each one of us is a specialist in her particular market. I am Executive Fashion Editor of Shoes and Stockings, and one time, lingerie, and before that, the accessories markets. A fashion editor should be better informed about her markets than any other person because she sees every line. Years spent in a market provides an editor with an invaluable background. She will know what has been done. She will also be well acquainted with the people in her markets. The fact that she has to call on the same people season after season makes her strive harder to be right about her selections.

Grace married, after the age of forty, to an attractive, delightful and brilliant man, Dr. William Cahan. He is a tremendous asset to the functions that he attends. We all love him. He is a charming host in his own home. They live in a beautifully decorated town house in the East 60's. Bill was Chief of Surgery, Thoracic Service, for the Sloan Kettering Memorial Hospital. He has helped many of us when we needed medical advice. Bill Cahan gives the impression of being a doctor who gives his patients understanding and assurance as well as excellent medical care. When I was looking for an arthritis specialist, he sent word by Grace that he would be glad to help me. Teddy Edelman had given me the name of Dr. Martin Meltger of the New York University Hospital, and I had gone to him. The right doctor for the right patient seldom happens. Dr. Meltger was the right doctor for me. Teddy had told him to level with me, tell me the truth so I would know what to expect. He was delightful from my first visit on. He said he wore his best suit, newest shirt, and favorite tie for me. This put me at ease and was amusing also.

At a later date, when I was discouraged and seemingly no better, he was superb. I told him that a friend had felt I was losing my self-esteem. He interrupted me and said, "You haven't lost your self-esteem; you are discouraged. You gave up too many things: Meat, wine, smoking, sex. I never told you to give up the wine or the sex." I laughed and said I could remedy the wine when I got home, but it wasn't that easy to find a man who wanted a 54-year-old crippled, ample woman with a new car, a pool that needed restoring and a dog with a bandage on his foot. He laughed. His easy, concerned attitude worked wonders with me. When I call he always comes on the phone. It is rare to find a doctor who gives so freely of his time. He insists that I check in several times a week, even when I am on vacation.

Grace became Editor-in-Chief and a bride during a short period of time. She seems capable of handling both, as well as an active social life. Grace and Beverly Sills were co-hostesses at a benefit for the New York City Opera. I went with Geoffrey Beene and was pleased and proud to see what a superb job Grace and Bill did as they went from table to table. They were both charming and had something to say to everyone present. A man sitting next to me was delighted by Grace and said as she left the table, "That's my kind of woman. What charm she has!" There are times when I feel the entire staff could leave without it affecting Grace. She has the capacity for not getting her emotions too involved with the editors who surround her. It isn't that she doesn't care, but rather a remoteness that protects her.

Anyone who needs praise, acclaim and reassurance should not become an editor. When Mrs. Vreeland was in charge, I came to the conclusion that being mature was being capable of knowing when you were good without anyone telling you. It must come from the gut, and that must suffice. Like an actress you are on the firing line, but without reviews. Also, an editor of *Vogue* has all the disadvantages of being well-known, a celebrity of sorts without many of the pluses.

At times I get a little disenchanted with Grace, especially when she is pulled in many directions. Quick decision-making is not one of her longsuits, but then I work on committees with other editors, and once again I am high on Grace's team.

Foreign
Photographic Trips

Why would a fashion editor go to far out, exotic and at times dangerous places for the purpose of bringing authenticity to her pictures? When I took the trips it is possible that I did not give enough thought to such matters or that I wanted the best and I couldn't settle for less. Whatever the reason, I traveled all over the world in hopes of bringing something extra to my pages in *Vogue*, and seldom, if ever, did I think of the consequences. I was young and I was fired with a passion to discover what happened in other cultures, how they lived, how they thought. There was a hope that some of the things I saw and experienced would rub off on me and add dimension to my life, as well as my pages.

Helen Keller said it best in this quote of hers from *The Open Door*:

> "Security is mostly a superstition. It does not exist in nature, nor do the children of men as a whole experience it. Avoiding danger is no safer in the long run than outright exposure. Life is either a daring adventure, or nothing. Serious harm, I am afraid, has been wrought to our generation by fostering the idea that they would live secure in a permanent order of things. They have expected stability and find none within themselves or in their universe. Before it is too late they must learn and teach others that only by brave acceptance of change and all-time crisis-ethics can they rise to the height of superlative responsibility."

ITALY

In 1956 I asked Joe Leombruno, a photographer of Italian descent who had never been to Italy, if he would like to go on a location trip to Bologna, Florence, and Rome. Joe worked with a partner, Jack Bodi, but it was decided that due to other pressing commitments only Joe would go on the trip.

The Italians were making beautiful shoes. Only a very few of them were making their way to America; not nearly enough better designer shoes were available in the states. They were made on Italian "lasts" that were not suitable for the American foot. The European foot is usually A, B, C, or D width and the American foot at that time was AA, A, or B. I asked Saks Fifth Avenue and Neiman Marcus if they would buy the shoes that we photographed, and they agreed to do so. The Bologna Shoe Fair was still small enough to be held in one large historic building. Today it is an enormous affair, so large that when I was there in March I couldn't even find the Director's office.

The plan was to cover the fair at which time I would select the most interesting, fashionable and prophetic shoes. We would hire models there and make our pictures. Things did not go too easily in the beginning. The shoes were beautiful, and that part of the job was rather simple. We even found several good models who could fit into the sample shoe sizes, but there were numerous ratty little problems. The models had hair on their legs, and they refused to shave them. They felt that hair made their legs sexier, and there seemed no way to persuade them that the hairs would soon grow again. No picture could be made with these legs and, if made, could not be published. After several days we left Bologna with the shoes and went to Florence where we made a few still life pictures without legs.

From there we traveled on to Rome where we found an American model who happened to be there on vacation. We knew her, told her of our plight, and asked if she would like to have a few days work. She had worked for Joe and Jack in New York and liked them, so she joined our group. We were behind schedule and in order to make our deadline we needed to work furiously. There was no time to go through official channels to get a permit each time we changed our location. We tried at first, but soon found that the endless red tape, explanation and waiting was too time consuming. It was also unfair, since any tourist can snap pictures at will without interference.

A routine was soon devised so that we could proceed. When police came while we were shooting and asked for our permit, Joe would finally tell them to see me. I fumbled through my bag, then the car and finally concluded it must be in the model's handbag. Joe continued taking his pictures until the law became disgruntled and demanded that we hand over the film. We tried to dissuade them. When that seemed impossible, we reluctantly gave up the film. Naturally, it was not the roll we had just shot. We kept an unused roll of film with the seal broken so it looked as though it had been used. It was our belief that the Italians would not waste the money to develop the blank film and apparently we guessed correctly. The procedure worked well. We completed our work, and came home with strong and dramatic pictures which appeared in the June, 1956 issue of *Vogue*.

Saks Fifth Avenue and Neiman Marcus kept their word, and the five Bologna designers whose shoes were used became successful in the American market. Both stores sold their shoes well and continued to do business with these Bologna manufacturers. Each time I returned there, the five original designers used in our pictures appeared richer and more prosperous. One attractive young designer, long on talent and short on funds, was riding a bicycle on our first trip. He graduated to a motor bike; a small car came next, then a large luxury car. It did my heart good to see him blossom.

In 1959, I returned to Italy with plans to attend the Bologna Shoe show. I had planned to take the nine a.m. train from Florence. When I woke I realized it was Sunday and I was tired. So why not sleep a little longer, take a later train? The most difficult lesson to learn on a foreign business trip is to find time to refuel oneself.

There were several friends from New York on the later train that arrived around noon, so we decided to go to one of Bologna's excellent restaurants and have a pleasant lunch.

The food was superb, the wine delicious; so we lingered, enjoying our Sunday lunch and good conversation.

Finally, I excused myself from my friends and made my way up the numerous steps of the old Palace where the show was held in order to pay my respects to the fair's Director. As I walked through the building people seemed to stare at me, but I dismissed the whole thing as my imagination and headed for the Director's office. When I opened the door I found the room filled with people whose faces seemed tired, worn, and bored. The Director became all smiles as he greeted me. He shook my hand, made a twelve minute speech in Italian, French, and English and I was handed a bronze statue mounted on a green marble base. The statue and its container weighed almost a hundred pounds and its weight caused me to fall on my face as the photographers' bulbs flashed. Three men hastened to help me to my feet, and the ceremony was repeated — all three translations. They told me that the press and a small band had met the nine a.m. train from Florence to welcome me. The entire group had been kept waiting all this time for my arrival. One can imagine how irritated they must have been. Someone should have spilled the beans and warned me. They explained that the award was the only one of its kind ever given. It was in recognition for bringing Italian shoes to America, but actually it was for doing a story that brought ten million dollars in business from the U.S. to the Bologna shoe manufacturers in one year. They sent the award to New York so that it would be there when I returned.

It was a distinction, and *Vogue* was pleased, but, through an error in judgement, or just not knowing, the name of *Vogue* wasn't mentioned on the silver plaque. There was nothing to be done. They had kept their secret almost too well. For the rest of my trip in Italy I avoided the newsstands. The pictures were printed in the papers and with the dark Italian ink they made me look like a gangster. I love Italy, the Italians, and after all these years, I have many Italian friends. Joe Leombruno and Jack Bodi later moved to Italy and they lived there for a number of years. They had a knitwear business that made beautiful young clothes. They lived in the Italian countryside and seemed to enjoy it tremendously.

TURKEY
    Since I was a child I have listened to adults talk about fighting in the Balkan, numerous wars between Turkey and Russia, and the Crimean War, when the free world came to the aid of Turkey. War has always been an unpleasant subject to me, but not Turkey.

I was intrigued by the mention of Turkey, its jewels, palaces, its mystique. In March 1965, Art Kane, an accomplished photographer, and I, along with a crew, went to Turkey to photograph a fashion story that appeared that year in the July issue of *Vogue* under the title "Turkerie."

It was a period in fashion when the metallics, especially gold, silver and bronze, were smart and appealing. The subtitle of the *Vogue* story was: "Turkerie: The Blaze and Lure of Seraglio Colours ... Shimmering Gold, Silver ... Slippers Like Scimitars ... Harem Sandals, Bare, Jewelled."

I enjoyed preparing for this trip. I studied as many books as I could to find and select beautiful patterns from the blue mosques to be used for tights. The lushness of the clothes, shoes and tights that we photographed fascinated me: gold jodhpur boots, gold harem tights, Retrousse sandals in jade silk with arabesques of carved stones. It was an exciting story; we were making the pictures in Turkey, and I had a great appreciation for the superb talents of Art Kane, a man capable of inexplicable compassion and sophistication in his pictures. Amid all this glitter, he sought the seamy side of life; he could take a broken down shack and give it dimension and style. We had worked together on a number of stories, but never on location.

Very few fashion editors had gone to Turkey for fashion sittings; however, several photographers had worked there, and they found the going rather tough. Conditions had improved somewhat but little did we know how difficult it would be. Whenever we did a set-up, people surrounded us. By the time we were ready to take the picture we were mobbed. It became impossible and rather dangerous and claustrophobic; so we had to transport our clothes and backgrounds to the country, away from the people.

The Turkish Tourist Bureau provided us with an aide who obtained permission for us to work in several of the fabulous old palaces that were filled with exquisite furnishings. We spent long hours walking through these lavish breathtakingly beautiful buildings. A few of them were at one time private homes. The opulence thrilled us - the shimmering crystal chandeliers, fabulous carpets, oversized brilliant precious stones, their extravagant furnishings -

and they would take us away from the crowds that had almost crushed us. There was one drawback, however. They were not heated and the weather was below freezing. No model could work there, change her clothes many times, sit for long periods of time without catching a cold, so we reluctantly concluded that we must forego working in all these imagined wonders.

Art thought we should use the oversized muscle-bound wrestlers with their bald heads, mustaches and gleaming, oiled bodies as a background, but I wasn't yet ready to do that. They seemed far too strong and overpowering and their appearance turned me off.

One evening we returned to the Istanbul Hilton, cold, tired, weary, aggravated and defeated. We were overwhelmed by the absurdity of our situation. I am sure more than one of us felt a little homesick. When we finished dinner our Turkish guide, hoping to cheer us up somewhat, suggested that we go to see the belly dancers. No one seemed to care one way of the other, so he took us to a nightclub that turned out to be less than aesthetic. Drugs were sold openly and tough men with gold teeth and big moustaches sat waiting for the show and anything else that came their way.

We endured the depraved surroundings for what seemed an eternity. Our emotions fluctuated from fear to amusement at the absurdity of finding ourselves here in this depressing atmosphere, especially after our unrewarding day. At long last, the dancers appeared and they weren't even belly dancers. They were Flamenco dancers imported from Spain.

The next day the guide introduced us to a well-known Turkish movie actress and her manager. They heard the story about our disappointing evening, and the manager offered to take us to the truly authentic belly dancers who lived in the ancient crumbling walls on the outskirts of Istanbul. He told us to meet him at an appointed place at midnight. We were to bring with us a large basket of fruit, two bottles of anisette and fifty dollars of small denominations in Turkish money. If we agreed he would make an appointment with the queen of belly dancers, and take us to her. Art has a huge capacity for adventure, so we went. The entire experience was unique and unforgettable.

Entire families made their homes in these damp, windowless walls. It was unbelievable to even imagine people living this way; yet, the makeshift rooms were neat and orderly. The mother sent the children out of the room. She and her husband supplied the music while three sisters started their competitive dances. Each one vied for our attention and the money we had been told to dole out to them. The dancers seemed exhilarated by their famous audience — Americans and their own most famous movie star. They adored the competition and seemed to become more stimulated rather then exhausted by their performance. Neither of them paid any attention to the women, but they adored Art, the attractive and famous American photographer, who could immortalize them in his pictures. Part of their ceremony was to continue their grinds and wiggles while they sat in the men's laps. Poor Art didn't feel well for many days.

During the evening we told the actress about our location problems and she suggested that we go to an ornate coffee house outside the walls, overlooking the Bosphorous. The next day we sought it out and found it interesting and workable.

Art Kane is an appealing man with a good sense of humor and a talent for adding a light touch to a heavy scene. He plays classical guitar and, fortunately, he took his guitar on the trip. His playing pulled us through long hours of waiting in airports.

After we had finished our work in and around Istanbul, we flew to Ephesus to photograph against the backgrounds of the Roman ruins of the fabulous marble city.

When we completed the Ephesus pictures, Art and I flew back to Manhattan. The rest of the crew went in different directions for a small holiday. Art had to get the film developed, and I had a deadline to make.

There are four main parts to a location trip for an editor: she must do the market work in order to get the fashion items, make a story and sell it to the powers that be, take the photographic trip, and be available to follow the story through the layouts and copy stage.

PERU

Marie Louise de Benavides and I are twins. We share the same birthday and we were born the same year. Neither of us knows the exact hour. She is half French, half Swedish, and she is married to a rich famous Spaniard. At times she will begin a sentence and I can finish it, or the other way around. We met in Lima, Peru when Norman Parkinson and I went to her home to photograph her large dramatic red parrots.

In 1966, Norman Parkinson, the well-known and distinguished English photographer, and I went to Peru to do a fashion story for the July issue of *Vogue* called "Inca-Metrics." It was an absorbing and unusual trip. Parkes, Bart Howard (the composer of *Fly Me To The Moon* and a personal friend) and I went ahead of the crew, so that we could pre-edit our camera shots. After Lima, we went to Cuzco and then Machu Picchu. At that time it was necessary to fly a small plane that provided the much needed oxygen through a tube in your mouth.

We were told, because of the altitude, to take things easy for the first twenty-four hours, to walk slowly, eat lightly and omit alcoholic drinks. Naturally we did not take things easy, so we felt the fatigue that was a result of thin air. The small hotel was rather primitive. At night when the temperature dropped, we were given no heat because it ate up too much oxygen. When I returned from the trip I had liquid in my lungs.

After Cuzco we took the three-hour, one-car-electric auto to Machu Picchu. The distance is seventy-five miles of enchanting adobe farm houses, awesome canyons, rich lush jungles and then the bus rides up to the magnificent ruins of the hidden city itself. The Incas had a genius for architecture. They chose an aesthetically appealing location, and having done this, they used nature to their advantage. One can still see in the ruins where there were fantastically designed farming terraces, a horse shoe shaped watchtower, gabled houses - all overlooking the lush, awesome valley below.

Parkes, Bart, and I were exhilarated by the trip to Cuzco and Machu Picchu; however, we found it too difficult and time consuming to bring the crew, the models might find the high altitude too restricting. Instead, we worked around Lima, in the desert, in the mountains, in people's homes and in Trujillo, a city to the north where we were told that the ambiance was still the way it was in viceregal days.

As is my custom, before a trip, I had done research on the ruins of Peru. Near Trujillo is an important ruin, Chimu at Chan. Parkes and I insisted that we see it. It is an eleven mile square area filled with remains of palaces and temples. We photographed at Chimu for hours, and one picture clearly shows the same design in the model's knee sock as in the ruins. I had given this design (found in a reference book on Peru) to a hosiery mill, and they had captured it beautifully. Secretly, I thanked the ancient Incas for their superb sense of design.

Trujillo had a dry, barren desert landscape except for the heart of the city where water had been brought down from the mountains to make a little vegetation possible. I was told that it had not rained there for twenty-five years. It staggers the mind.

One of the most awesome and disturbing sites on the outskirts of Trujillo was a small deserted cemetery sitting on the shady side of a crumbling little church that was bleached and peeling from exposure to the blistering sun. It rested in dark black sand that was blown and scattered by the winds, left to parch on a hill just a few hundred yards from the sea. Small bits of lusterless tinsel, faded artificial flowers and leftovers from a withered wreath blew aimlessly over the grave markers fighting to withstand the sandstorms, but failing miserably in their struggle. Not a blade of grass, or even a tired worn out weed could be seen. The desolation, isolation, despair and a deafening silence hurt my ears and tugged at my emotions. I made an effort to get away from these death signs that were chilling the marrow of my bones, but my feet seemed glued to the scorched wasteland. I felt transfixed, unable to shake off the depression that surrounded, and suffocated me.

Finally, we left and drove to the small airport to take our flight back to Lima, only to find that strong winds had cancelled the plane, and we were stuck for the night without clothes or cosmetics.

As our small group of six — two models, a photographer, assistant, hairdresser, and editor — sat there in the bleak cheerless excuse for an airport, the crippled, worn out venetian blinds flapped aimlessly in the wind. The ghostly graveyard kept gnawing at my insides. I knew how it must feel to be deserted and left at the last outpost. It is at a moment like this when one wonders if the work is really important, and if so, to whom. I thought of a loved one, wondered what I was doing so far from home.

An influential citizen of Trujillo, much taken by one of the models (who later married Ted Williams, the baseball hero), came to our rescue and helped us make the best of a bad situation. He arranged accommodations for us at a small hotel, brought us toothbrushes and other essentials and put together an old-fashioned barbecue (Texas-style) for the evening. Before the evening meal, which was held at a social, ranch-type club, he took us to his home near the heart of the city. As we walked into his courtyard, he reversed the iron-clad lantern that hung over the entrance. He explained this was to indicate, to others, that he had distinguished guests in his home. We were flattered. Little by little we began to discard our melancholy and enjoy what turned out to be a festive evening. Since there was but one plane a day we decided to use the next day to find and photograph interesting locations.

We took pictures of the long reed floats that the natives ride, like a horse, through the surf. This requires a special skill which only the natives seem to possess. We found brilliant zigs, marvelous zags, earth brown colors actually pre-Incan, golds silhouetted against the sweep of the Andes. The day turned out well and we left, this time on schedule, for Lima.

A travel guide from the Peruvian tourist bureau had told us about the fabulous Benavides home, its animals and Marie Louise, a woman loved and admired by all who knew her. A call was made to see if we could come there to take pictures. Marie Louise agreed to the arrangement; so, off we went to her home. Little did we know of the pleasant and rewarding experiences that lay ahead of us.

Marie Louise is a remarkable and intimate woman. She is quite beautiful, with deep watery blue eyes that show a compassion for mankind and all the earth's creatures. Her husband, Felipe's father, gave the Children's Zoo to Lima. They search for small abandoned animals, bring them into their large fenced-in estate and tame them as they grow. It is not unusual to find several capuchin monkeys, a leopard or two, one or more ocelots, eight or more macaws, a collection of cats, numerous dogs, and at least two hundred rare, beautiful red parrots living within their walls.

When Marie Louise was in Roxbury for a few days last year, she told me several interesting and touching stories about their animals. She had a young ocelot cub. This particular breed of cat was seldom known to be tamable. However, the Benavides had been able with patience and love to make friends with him. As he grew larger his claws also grew, and they cause a great deal of damage to furniture and to Marie Louise's clothing when the cat jumped up on her. One evening at a dinner party she told the story to a scientist sitting next to her. He listened intently, and then explained that, since the cat would eventually live in the zoo and have no need for such long claws for hunting, why not file them and his long teeth? He would be put to sleep so he would feel no pain. On the appointed day, Marie Louise took the cat in her car to the laboratory where the filing was done. The ocelot continued to have his place in the household and all seemed well. One day when Marie Louise was on the phone he came to her, jumped up in a friendly way (she explained that he usually acted this way in the early morning or in the evening) as if to say good-bye and walked away. When she finished her call and looked for the cat, he was gone. The servants and the entire household took up the search. They were distressed by his disappearance, and the search was continued for days. They knew that without his long claws and teeth, the cat could not hunt or protect himself. They even went into the mountains with chickens for food, trying to bring him out. Marie Louise spent two nights and days on the mountain. She believed that if he saw her, he would come to her. Everything failed until a man came to the house with news. He had seen the cat in the mountains with a female fox who was hunting and taking care of him. Several months later news came again. The fox and the cat were still traveling together. They were seen through binoculars, running through the mountains. It seems that the two strange bedfellows must have had an agreement. She thinks the fox visited their estate at some time, the two talked it over and the cat followed the fox. An odd couple, but what a tender story!

One time Marie Louise needed a doctor when her English physician was out of town. A well-known young Spanish doctor was called. He came and turned back the comforter on her bed. Sleeping between the lightweight down throw and the covers was an ocelot and three smaller animals. He was shocked. He didn't speak a word, just dropped the covers, walked out of the room, left the house and never contacted her again. It is unusual to have the animals as part of the household. The Benavides explained that they enjoy taming the animals and when tame, they seem better adjusted to the zoo and to the children. I have mixed and conflicting feelings about animals in zoos. However, we visited the Lima Children's Zoo, and I found that the animals were provided with adequate space and attention. Felipe's sister devotes most of her time to the animals' welfare.

The Benavides estate adjoins the golf course, and on rare occasions, an animal or two has been known to surprise golfers as the animals wander across the greens. One of the unusual household pets was a tapir, an animal indigenous to South America and not especially beautiful. They look something like a combination of an elephant and a pig. They grow to the size of a cow, but they are sweet, shy and gentle.

The tapir had a fondness for the drawing room fire, so when it was lit he made his way to the hearth. Guests who did not know about him were frequently caught off stride. One evening Felipe was entertaining a group of men at a formal dinner. The guest of honor was an English dignitary who had a tendency to discuss political controversies. Felipe called the butler and quietly asked him to open the door to the tapir's room. The animal walked through the dining room. No one looked surprised but the Englishman was shocked and stopped his conversation in mid-sentence.

The tapir got so large he could not get through the doorway, so he was taken to the zoo. When Marie Louise goes to the zoo in her rather old Mercedes, the tapir recognizes the sound of the engine. He breaks free from his yard and is always waiting to greet her when she gets out of the car.

ISRAEL

Peter Merom did a handsome book of photography on the landscape of Israel. The two college students who drove our cars, Gideon and Big Ben, presented it to me when we finished our work. Peter wrote a few significant lines for the introduction:

> "Within himself, every man has his own country. It is a land whose appearance he alone has formed, a personal illusion in which the actual dunes and mountains and waters mingle with the landscapes of imagination perceived only by himself. This is the land he loves. A land wholly and uniquely his. Here on these pages is my land."

Israel is almost too overpowering. It is many worlds blended together: Old Jerusalem, the Sea of Galilee, the Dead Sea, the Wailing Wall, and the bright, healthy, beautiful young people making their own new world. It's a country of contrasts and unexpected surprises, some good, some of necessity, too fierce.

The youth impressed me so much I took color pictures of them with my Minox camera. After I got home, away from the magic of the country, I wondered if they would still look so attractive. They did. I used the slides when I spoke at one of the Fashion Group's lecture series, and they still looked pink-cheeked and glowing.

They are outgoing and friendly. When we went to a night spot they came to our table to visit, talk, dance, and sing with us. Their enthusiasm and zest for life were infectious. Part of it must have come from living on the edge of war. The women serve in the army as well as the men. They pull out all the stops when they relax in a good watering spot. Strangely enough, they drink very little alcohol; instead they prefer orange juice because they feel they need good health and strong bodies.

Vogue did an important story on Israel in July, 1969. John Gowan, an English photographer, and I went there to work on it. He came from London, and I flew from New York. It was our plan to spend a few days together mapping out locations before the models and hairdressers arrived.

Armi Ratia flew from Finland to spend three days with John and me as we covered the small country. (John had been to Finland the winter before to photograph the Marimakko fashions for English *Vogue*, so he and Armi knew each other).

I flew on the Israeli airlines both ways even though it was during the peak of the high-jacking fever. The trip over was pleasant so I landed in Tel Aviv in good spirits, looking forward to discovering the country. Everything went well until I reached customs. Our broker in New York had sent ahead, in triplicate, a customs declaration of the fashions I was bringing into the country for photographic purposes only. The merchandise was sealed and bonded and each item, including jewelry, was itemized as to value. I had a list to accompany the clothes. We had taken every precaution. We do this so often we are very thorough.

The customs man read down my list until he came to a mink jacket. Immediately he closed the large black aluminum cases we use for travel, and said I would have to wait for his superior. Armi was at the airport so when I didn't come through the customs door she finally came looking for me.

After waiting more than two hours my patience was wearing thin, and I was exhausted from the long flight. Someone from the tourist bureau should have been there, but there was a mix-up. Finally I was cleared after waiting more than three wretched hours. I walked into the Tel Aviv Hilton to meet John Cowan, for the first time, and found him with one arm in a cast. The large box of film that I had brought for him was wrong in some mysterious way. It was what he had ordered.

The country was thrilling, so much so that my frustrations slipped away, and after a hot bath I was ready for the trip to Jerusalem. John had been earlier in the day, so he suggested we take a cab. The trip from Tel Aviv takes about an hour. We later hired two cars and two university students to drive and guide us. They told us about the country as they saw it, and one took us to his home in Northern Israel. It was a week before Easter, and the home was getting a coat of paint in preparation for the Easter celebrations.

Seeing Jerusalem for the first time was a deep and moving experience. When we arrived there it was close to twilight, bells were ringing, sounds of the chanting Arabs floated over the hills as they bowed facing Mecca. I was transfixed, caught up in Biblical times. It was as though my whole life had been leading up to this one overpowering moment. Jerusalem was steeped in history, past and present.

John stayed in Jerusalem that evening so Armi and I drove back to Tel Aviv together. Because we needed to come back to reality we began telling funny stories about ourselves. She told me that her divorce had become final a few weeks before. At the time she was in a Finnish village buying cotton fabric, and when she returned to the small, bare, still hotel room a phone call broke the silence and a voice on the other end of the line told her she was a single woman again. After thirty-five years of marriage she felt that there should be some celebration or dramatic happening, but she was away from home, sitting in a sad little room, alone except for the red roses someone had sent her.

She said her first reaction was to cry, but then she began thinking about her wedding night and she laughed.

Before the engagement was announced her husband-to-be, Vee Ratia, took her home to meet his mother. At this time Armi was a designer, but the mother asked that they call her a dressmaker in the newspaper. The word "designer" seemed too bold. It was decided that the wedding would be at Vee's home; Armi couldn't remember why. As is the custom at Finnish weddings, the guest list is long. After the ceremony there was much drinking and eating, so the dirty dishes began to pile up. The house had a small, seldom-used servants' bedroom by the kitchen.

It didn't have a proper mattress on the bed. Instead, the bed was piled high with straw. During the course of the evening, the servants had used this room to stack dirty dishes. They were piled on the bed and scattered on the floor. When time came for bed, the house guests were shown to their rooms. In the confusion of wedding preparations no one had thought about a room for the bride and groom; so Armi and Vee had to sleep in the room with all the dirty dishes, with straw for a mattress on their wedding night. We laughed so hard and so long that the two drivers in the front seat, who spoke no English, began laughing with us. What an electrifying day it had been.

The next day John and I flew to Eilat with our guide from the tourist bureau. There had been fighting in that southern part of the country, but we were told that everything was quiet. Eilat was a new city in the desert that was in the process of being built. We stayed in a nice modern hotel that was almost completed. The rooms were small but fresh white and clean. When I checked in I found that my door would not close. I asked a translator to tell the desk clerk; he did and the clerk just laughed. This seemed rather strange to me but I assumed the door would be fixed. We went out to dinner and then to a nightclub that was filled with marvelous singing happy voices. "Delilah" was a popular song at that time and they adored singing it. The evening was sensational. Students and soldiers came to our table and talked about what was happening in Israel. We danced and sang until the wee hours and then returned to our hotel. My door was still ajar so I just slept in my jeans and a sweater with the door open. It was too late to make other arrangements.

During the night there was firing across the bay of Eilat. When I arose in the morning I understood why the desk clerk had laughed. I had no door. There was also a long crack in the nice new wall of my room. It was easy to see why the young people had put so much into their evening.

The day's drive through the desert from Eilat back to Tel Aviv was colorful. We stopped at kibbutzes, found a thrilling sight for photography, saw large white birds so crowded into the few trees on the edge of the desert that they looked like massive white leaves. We were told that these birds in their migration north stop and nest in these same trees this time every year.

I was rather sunburned when we reached Tel Aviv. My hair and clothes were filled with sand, and my eyes were red. About halfway through the desert I learned to wear two pair of sunglasses to protect my eyes from the blowing hot sand.

The day before I left for Israel, I had broken a tooth and my dentist put on a temporary cap. I have good teeth. This was my first cap, so it did not occur to me that I might have trouble. During that memorable night in Eilat my cap had come loose. There was no dentist in the desert, so I had glued the cap on with Elmer's glue.

I went to a dentist in Tel Aviv. The hotel called and made the appointment. A cab took me for miles to a residential section where a dentist had a modern well-equipped office in his home. He spoke no English, so you can imagine his puzzlement when he found ordinary white glue holding the cap, not too well, to my tooth. There was no way to explain what had happened. He must have had strange misgivings about American dentists.

Francois Ilnseher, a superb hair dresser, has worked at Kenneth's and Suga's salons and is now a free-lancer on his own, working mostly on T.V. Some years back I went to him to get my own hair cut. He was at Kenneth's at the time. Soon afterward I asked him to work with me on a sitting. He comes from Switzerland, had worked in England, South Africa, and had plans to work his way around the world. I persuaded him to stay put, and go with me on foreign location trips. He can do anything, he enjoys keeping busy, so I used him as a hairdresser and an assistant. We are good friends and have traveled together in the U.S.A. and abroad. He went on the Peru and Israel trips, among others.

He and Dorothy, his attractive wife, have two small sons. They seem like family to me. One day a young editor from English *Vogue* who does the hosiery market was visiting my office. I showed her the fabulous hosiery we have in America, but she said nothing impressed her as much as Francois coming to my office to cut my hair. He either comes there or to my apartment. It is a great luxury for me. I don't have the patience to wait or sit under a dryer.

Francois is interested in everything. On a trip he washes the models' hair every night before they go to bed and puts it up in curlers. This keeps him up later than the rest of the group. After he finishes with the models' hair, he works on his wigs and hairpieces to be used the next day. Even so, he is up at dawn, to explore the country, meet the people and take his own pictures. A good hairdresser is invaluable, and Francois is the best with whom I've ever worked. He has a rare and wonderful talent for smoothing the rough edges during a trying day, and afterward when everyone is worn and anxious about the day's work. It's remarkable how seldom there are temper flares or cross words. We are there for the work; the quality of work affects each person's career; so we work hard and play hard when the work is finished.

AFRICA

I met Arthur Edelman and his wife Teddy when she was pregnant with their oldest child, Sam, who is now in business with *Esprit*.

When the shoe show was on in Chicago I usually took a suite at the Ambassador East. One evening I invited a group to join me for drinks and then took twenty-five to dinner. This was the largest number the Pump Room could seat at one long table that ran from one end of the room to the other. I tried asking more people for dinner, but no one was happy at the side tables.

This was a *Vogue* party, and we tried to have a mixed group of manufacturers, tanners, designers, and just friends. The cocktail party had a small orchestra and at least two hundred more guests than were invited. Everyone had a guest or a friend and felt free to bring them. It didn't really matter except when the suite got too crowded.

The party was going along well when a tall, six-foot, six-inch dramatic man walked in. He had heard that *Vogue* was giving a party; so he came. I liked him immediately, but his oversized feet kept

66

knocking over glasses as he became more lubricated. Finally, one of the men from *Vogue* decided to help Arthur to the elevator. He went nicely. He was pleasant, charming, but each time a new guest arrived he came back with him. The trip to the elevator was attempted at least five times, and I got rather nervous for fear his feelings would be hurt. Two hours later when I came down the elevator with my date for dinner (this was before the Pump Room parties) Arthur was propped up against the elevator, waiting to invite me to dinner. We have been good friends since that day. I love Arthur, Teddy, and their family of six children.

Arthur had been an actor before he joined Fleming Joffe, tanners of reptiles and owned by Morris Joffe, Teddy's father. He literally learned the business from the bottom up, working in the basement with the salt bins where the skins are salted down, and eventually became President of the firm.

Teddy came to work with Arthur soon after he started. They were good at their jobs. They planned colors and were very interested in promotion. One day when I was working with them in their office (this was before many reptiles were placed on the endangered list) Arthur said, "Why don't we go on a trip to Africa?"

The idea was discussed with Alexander Liberman and Mrs. Vreeland, and the trip was planned. Gordon Parks seemed a logical choice for photographer, and why not take his attractive second wife, Liz, as the model. Arthur found a white hunter who knew the territory. So off we went to Zambia. At that time it was Northern Rhodesia, Southern Rhodesia, and Kenya. What a group: a white hunter from Ceylon, a black photographer and his half-black wife, a Southern editor, a Jewish reptile man and a black driver.

This was before the time of the 747 planes; so Gordon, Liz, Arthur and I flew to London and stayed the night. Next morning we boarded a B.O.A.C. jet, and twenty-three hours later we landed at Livingston Airport in Northern Rhodesia. We had stopped at Rome, Khartoum; changed planes at Kenya and had a three hour wait. It was snowing when we left London and over a hundred degrees when we landed at our final destination.

Gordon Parks is a man for all seasons. He is a photographer, and accomplished musician. He has composed several concertos which have been performed in New York, Munich and Venice. He had written *The Learning Tree*, his first book about his life, which later became a movie for which he wrote the screenplay, the music and produced and directed the film.

At the time of our trip he was working on the second book about his life *A Choice of Weapons*. I sat next to him on the long plane trip and watched him write and suffer as he relived the despair and oppression of his earlier days.

In the foreword of *Born Black*, a late book of essays commissioned by *Life*, he says:

> "I came to each story with a strong sense of involvement, finding it difficult to screen out my own memories of a scarred past. But I tried for truth, the kind that comes through looking and listening, through the careful sifting of day-to-day emotions that white America whips up in black people. My own background has enabled me, I hope, to better share the experiences of some other black people. I do not presume to speak for them. I have just offered a glimpse, however fleeting, of their world through black eyes."

Gordon has been close to my heart since the day, years ago when he walked into my office. I had seen his work in *Life* on poetry. He had an ingredient in his work, a tenderness, that touched me, made me long to work with him. I asked Alex if it were possible to get Gordon for my next assignment of pages. He made the arrangement and an appointment was set up for the meeting. The first time I knew Gordon was a black man was when he walked into my office. It made not the slightest difference to me. I saw a great humanity, and a depth of feeling in his face. He is also a very handsome man.

We talked and I asked him if he had done much fashion photography. He had worked with Sally Kirkland, then the fashion editor of *Life*, and said that he had been called by another fashion magazine, but they weren't interested when they found out he was black. This upset me so that I invited him to Roxbury to work from my house. I had tried to keep work separate from the house, but this was different. He came and did a fantastic job, and we worked together numerous times after that day.

Gordon owned a home in White Plains where he also had a studio. We did several assignments there, but he preferred working with natural light, always late in the afternoon after the harsh rays of the sun had quieted.

In addition to the White Plains house, he kept an apartment on Beekman Place, across the street from my apartment. He was a good neighbor. When I came from the hospital, after an operation, and was not permitted to drive to the country on the weekends, he often cooked for me on Sunday evening in his beautiful apartment on the top floor of a brownstone house. I saw him regularly and still see him. He now lives in the U.N. Plaza. We often meet on the street when he is in town. I saw him on Beekman Place a few days ago and asked him about his tennis. He said, "I'm an adequate photographer, musician, writer and movie maker, but I consider myself a superb tennis player."

The African trip lasted almost a month and was fraught with traumas. We spent long hours traveling through the two Rhodesias editing out the things that a tourist might see. We found some interesting native paintings on the walls of a Makishi village, and asked if we might be allowed to photograph a group of native fertility dancers. Permission was granted. We were told to return in five days when everything would be ready. We left and returned on the appointed day. No preparations had taken place, and we had wasted too much time to go away empty handed.

Each time I go on a trip to a foreign country I do my homework by reading everything I can find about the country, its people, their habits. I knew that this tribe sometimes paint their legs for the fertility dance; so I asked if I might be allowed to paint the legs of two native men. Fortunately in my large cosmetic bag I had clown make-up brought for an unexpected occasion. A group of native boys looked me over carefully, then refused. A few extra coins helped persuade two of them to agree to the procedure. I don't think these natives

69

believed in baths. The day was hot. Finally, the unpleasant task was completed not one minute too soon for me or them. I made purple rings followed by white just as a reference book had said it should be, from their ankles to above their knees, and we were ready for the pictures to be made. No dancing took place, and Gordon asked the interpreter why there was a delay. It was explained that more money was required, a local orchestra was needed, and they must have time for their drugs to take effect. At long last the shooting took place and we set out for a restaurant on the Sambesi river for a dinner party.

The mayor of Livingston and a group of distinguished citizens were having a dinner for us. When they invited us I explained that we would be delighted to come if a place could be chosen that would permit us to come directly from work in our safari clothes. We arrived at six o'clock at their picturesque setting, a large table outside overlooking the river that was populated by hippopotamus and other interesting animals. The mayor congratulated me on my engagement to two Makishi boys. It had come in on the drums. He explained that the painting of the legs was an engagement ceremony. We were scheduled to fly the next day to Kenya; so we left, but not before we got the lion picture.

Our small but dauntless group had trekked through the rain forest of Central Africa, repulsed a raiding party of dog-faced baboons, boated on the Sambesi where alligators pounded on the bottom of our small boat, but we didn't yet have a good picture of a lion. Two days before we had gone to a large game preserve where we were told a lion and his lioness came to eat. We did the set-up for our picture. The grass was dry and parched; so we kept buckets filled with flowers. I had taken from New York two large pillows with suede covers. We put three stone colored alligator shoes on a red pillow and placed large amounts of meat behind the pillow. The plan was for the lion to rush for the meat and the picture would be made with him in the background. We waited, and waited. It seems two-thirds of a location trip is spent waiting for the hairdresser to do the model's hair, set up for the photographer, good weather, the sun to set, travel, waiting for planes and more of the same.

The lion and his mate finally came. He does not allow her to approach until he has eaten. Instead of stopping at the meat, he rushed to the pillow, ate the shoes, completely ignoring the raw meat, and left — but not before he had ripped the suede cover on both sides with his sharp claws. I brought this pillow home along with its ripped red cover. It rests behind the iron chaise in my Roxbury living room. I put another cover over the one the lion tore, to protect it.

We were crestfallen not to have gotten the lion pictures. As we drove the long miles back to our hotel in Southern Rhodesia, we decided to try again in two days. A lion eats every two days. Fortunately, shoes come in pairs, so we had the other shoe, and I had brought duplicate pillow covers.

On our departure day we prepared our set-up, again waited and finally the lion and his mate arrived. Gordon was able to snap only one picture before he had to run like hell, climb the fence and flee. Even though we got only one print (normally we would have taken four or five rolls in color and the same in black and white), *Vogue* printed the picture as a two page spread in color. It was slightly blurred, but that added to its reality. There was no way that picture could have been faked.

The lion's face is compelling; his eyes reach out to you, and his huge head is majestic and powerful looking. Every time I see the picture the sweetness of its beauty brings tears to my eyes.

We left for Nairobi where we stayed several days, rented a zebra striped Volkswagen bus and set off for Carr Hartley's 32,000 acre game preserve in the upper part of the Rift Valley.

We were in Nairobi shortly after Kenyatta came into power. It was an interesting time; but we had to be careful of what we said. The country was still nervous. There was a correspondent from *Life*, a man who had been born in India, who took us around. He introduced us to the native artists, showed us the English schools that Kenyatta had taken over and explained this was the first time natives had been allowed to come to Nairobi and stay overnight. We were surprised and delighted to see a large window in a Nairobi bookstore given over to *The World in Vogue*. Jessica Daves and Alexander Liberman had

71

only recently sent this book to press, and I hadn't seen a finished copy. How often we are reminded of the smallness of the world in which we live. The book window was a pleasant reminder of home.

The political atmosphere was somewhat hairy when we were in Rhodesia. Northern Rhodesia, now Zambia, had acquired its independence only two months before we arrived. Our hotel was in Southern Rhodesia, but the town of Livingston, the game preserves — both countries share the magnificent Victoria Falls, but our approach was in Northern Rhodesia — native villages, rain forest, and airport were in Northern Rhodesia. Each time we crossed the border it was necessary to go through two inspections — car, personal property, papers and passports — on the trip across and again two more inspections on the trip back. It was a bore. We transported clothes, shoes, accessories, cameras, film, cosmetics and food. We had to allow a minimum of an hour each way — two precious hours wasted each time we crossed the borders.

The white hunter was slightly wild. He was left with long waiting periods while we photographed; so he thought up excursions for us. He enticed us to take a midnight ride on the Zambesi River. Gordon and Liz had better sense, but Arthur and I went. Arthur started the trip and I was to meet them at a given point about and hour later. They arrived, and I was surprised to find that the motor boat was rather small and without a light, except for the miner's hat that was on the white hunter's head. Perhaps I should explain that Arthur had chosen a white hunter who knew the reptile market and could help him buy alligators while he was in Africa. This wild, insane man is in no way indicative of the usual capable and reliable men who lead safaris.

Arthur looked a little pale when he came into the car lights. That should have warned me, but apparently it did not; so off I went in this small boat with a madman who was also a speed demon. Alligators and hippopotamuses and heaven knows what else hit against the bottom and sides of the boat, and on we sped with little or no light and less brains.

We may have never been heard from again if the boat hadn't eventually run out of gas. This was a relief, but it kept us from returning to the car. We worked our way to the river bank and waited.

The wait was frightening because we had so little light and no way to avoid stepping on snakes and other dangerous animals that frequent the Zambesi River bank. Some time later — it seemed like an eternity — Arthur and the driver found us.

Thank God, I am now not so young or foolish as I was in those earlier days.

It was impossible to take food along on the trip up the Rift Valley; so we drove until we found an inn or anything close to an inn. We stopped and waited while they cooked for us.

Carr Hartley has a home in the heart of this game preserve, and a Turkana tribe makes their home on this land. They eat no meat. Their entire diet consists of blood and milk. They get the blood from the cattle. The women wear no clothes, except for the numerous beads around their necks.

Liz dressed in our bus and the women were all eyes. They have little or no hair on their heads, and they could not understand why Liz put hair on her head and smaller hair on her eyelashes. Her wigs puzzled them.

Even though their women are almost naked, neither the men nor the boys seem to look at them. It was amusing to go into a museum in Livingston and see the boys stare at the bare mannequins, and point and snicker. They could see the real thing on the street but they were too polite to look.

Carr Hartley had a large female elephant that was used in one of our pictures. She seemed nice and gentle, and Arthur dared me to ride her, bareback no less. Silly fool that I was, I allowed several men to give me a push on her back. It never occurred to me that she would be covered with mud, so my clothes were ruined. No sooner had I gotten settled, when she took off running, as fast as she could, for the bush, with me holding on to her ears. The natives and helpers followed in their landrovers.

How in the hell was I going to get down off a huge running elephant? My eyes searched for a branch of a tree. There were trees, here and there, but they turned out to be thorn trees covered with long sharp thorns. After what seemed a lifetime, the elephant men caught and quieted her, and I managed to get to the ground.

Carr gave me a few pointers about how to handle wild animals. He said, "Never take your eye off the animal. Stare him down, hold your ground, and do not act frightened."

He had a leopard in his preserve in a cage. They had become friends, and he enjoyed standing outside the cage talking to the cat while he rubbed her head. One time when he was doing this someone called Carr by name. He turned his head to answer the call, and the cat bit off the middle and second fingers of his right hand. Had he not taken his eyes away from the animal, he says, it would not have happened.

I adore animals; so Africa was thrilling to me. I cannot bear to think of them being shot just for sport. We saw great herds of zebra. They are timid and frightened at the least disturbance. They sometimes trample each other as they flee from something that frightens them.

The giraffe feed mostly on thorn trees. I can't imagine why the thorns don't stick as they slide down their long necks.

The laughing hyena came close to where we were working, walked away, then returned time and again. We seemed to fascinate them. Little wonder.

Gordon and I were both injured during a shooting in the upper Rift Valley. Everything was going well, when it looked like rain. There was a group of ten native women and one native man with us. These natives don't like to get even a drop of water on them. I hurried to get the next outfit out of the truck so that Liz might make her change before the rain came. Our driver, in his rush, forgot to lock the back door to the bus when he lifted it for me to reach the clothes. It dropped, hit me on the back of the head and I was out for a few minutes.

Shortly afterwards, during the same sitting, Gordon was trying to put the native women at ease. They were a little stiff, and a man from their tribe was there to watch over them. They carried chains around their middle, attached to a hard metal round object. Gordon danced around with them, and they joined in, swinging these heavy metal objects at the most personal parts of Gordon's anatomy. One hit him, and I saw him pale and go down on his knees. This ended the frolic for him, but the women began to fight among themselves. We later learned that the one who hit him was supposed to get him. Can't imagine what good he would have done her.

As we drove back about a hundred and fifty miles to the closest inn where we got our evening meal and lodging, Gordon and I were feeling a little the worse for wear. However, we got up the next morning, returned to the game preserve, and completed the job.

Liz and Gordon flew to Switzerland. Arthur and I flew back to New York. *Vogue* asked Gordon to write something about the trip for the travel pages that appeared in the same issue as the fashion pages. The fashion feature was called "The Day of the Reptile."

I would like to share with you Gordon's account of our plane trip to Africa. It appeared in the July 1964 issue.

Flight Over Africa by Gordon Parks

"Over Ismaill, Aswan, Toski, Wadi Half, Abu Hamed, Dongola, and Shendi we flew, it seemed, faster than sound, splintering the silence of mysterious African night, pushing time, intercepting hours yet unlived in Kansas, Minnesota, or Texas. Paris and Rome lay far behind as we streaked high above the Nubian Desert heat. A moment of confusing light shone far below — the moon shimmering on the twisting Nile. The stars moved with us, accompanied our long descent toward Khartoum, lying small, jewel-like in the immeasurable blackness.

"We banked steeply into the dark and suddenly Khartoum, withdrawn into itself a few moments before, was rushing up to welcome us. We greeted it with yawning eyes. The airport was alive with the white-robed and ebony-skinned whose indulgent eyes drew us out. We looked of the West, strangers to their heat, desert, colour, and talk. So many stars between us. So many empty spaces for bush to grow and sands to roll.

"We, not they, were on display, and discomfort turned us to the trinkets and wares. As they were of no worth, there was no reward for the hawkers who stayed awake.

"Airborne again. The world tilted as we shot swiftly into the upper skies toward Nairobi and morning. Then, far below to the left, a ball of red sun, big in the approaching dawn, moved up from the horizon, and proving its ageless sovereignty, spiked unmerciful heat into a sandstorm that churned the desert for as far as the eye could see. Pity for those caught in the evil of the haboob's fierce beauty.

"There, miles below, stopped where the long brown river snaked out from the desert, were two camels and their riders — stopped where there was every good reason to stop. They crouched between their animals just before the mountain of black sand blotted them from our view. One could only speak to God for them. Now, Senner, Malakal, Jinja, and Entebbe. Next, Mounts Kenya and Kilimanjaro envying one another's majesty.

"On southward, pillaged and evangelized for mortal stakes, Kenya's wilderness, strung out in all faraway directions; holding tribes, rites, and customs that stream through backward time; harboring things long fearsome to man, jungle, leopard, lion, and cobra. A sun glint summoned the eye beneath a cloud break and there, speaking the future, was Nairobi.

"We go in noisily, jarring hostile animals' ears. Nairobi, tolerable hot, filled with Africans, Indians, a sprinkling of British doggedly holding on, sipping tea of colonial afternoons, proclaiming right, fingering wrong, acknowledging, painfully, the current now running strongly from native source.

"The Rhodesias lie another three hours ahead. We roared down the runway and lifted off, our quake scattering a herd of giraffe into ridiculously graceful loping several miles beyond the clearing. Wembere, Steppe, Tabora, Mpwaspa to our left; Ujiji, Nyangwe, the Lualaba River far beyond the clouds to our right. And though blood spilled as we burst over the plains of Tanganyika, our air was full of peace. The slaughter belonged to them below, whoever they were. Such height as ours lay grief and concern to rest. We had not come to fight or die.

"Nor could the motel at Victoria Falls be kept waiting. Several hippos, bubbling in the slow moving Zambesi River, dived from our noise. A pair of otters and more dangerous than they appeared, crouched in the shade of a monkey tree. We were at journey's end now and Livingston's Africa was opening beneath us like a giant flower. But like a melting mountain, the awesome fall of Victoria emptied unsparingly in its valley of constant rain.

"That night, after a sunset only a poem could tell, a huge single star, hypnotic, brilliant, and unbelievable, hung moon-bright over the black Zambesi, shimmering the water. Things said of such beauty seem weak. Only the traveller's eye can know the truth — and perhaps, lock it in the memory."

Edna Woolman Chase

Jessica Daves

Diana Vreeland

Alexander Liberman

Kay Hays - Early Days at Vogue

Gordon Parks and Kay Hays - Helsinki Airport

Kay Hays at work

Gordon Parks

Norman Parkinson

How One Fashion Editor Spends Her Time

The life of a fashion editor is compelling, varied, absorbing, demanding, exasperating, perhaps frivolous, uncertain, rewarding. Each editor finds her own way of working. She adjusts her hours, usually long and well into the evening, to what makes her the most productive. At all times she must have an open understanding mind, a warm receptive heart, the ability to edit without offending.

At collection time or market week as some refer to the showings of a new season, editors work not only days and evenings but through the weekend. On Wednesday I flew to Milan. A car and driver met me and we drove for three hours to Bologna for the Spring Shoe Show. This show is the first weekend in September for spring fashions, and the first weekend in March, either in Milan or Bologna, for fall fashions. I stay in Bologna until Monday when I fly in a small cramped plane either to London or   Paris where I work for two or three days with designers. From the time the plane leaves New York until it sets down at Kennedy Airport a week later I will have absolutely no free time and not too much sleep. Every meal is planned, every hour is taken. If all goes well the trip will be exhausting, stimulating, fulfilling. Seldom do I find the news and excitement needed to fill my part of the pages of *Vogue*. After the extensive coverage is done, in my case I've taken about two months to see lines from all my important people, my job is just beginning. I cover New York shows in August and February, preceding the Italian shows for the same season.

With the exception of the month of July when I am in Roxbury and Block Island on my holiday, I go at a steady pace every month.

There is no way anyone, including me, can actually do my job — like the old joke about Vermont, you can't get there from here. Today at *Vogue*, we have three major sitting editors: Polly Melon, Jade Hahson, Carlyne Serf. Each of them has different taste about shoes. I must please myself first, then Grace Mirabella and each of them. Jade likes simpler, understated, more classic shoes that are closer to the ground. Carlyne is especially attracted to high heels, jazz, unusual, far-out styles. Polly is more open, more receptive to change. She has a rare gift for using the new, special, unexpected things, as well as the casual conventional styles. In my opinion, Polly

Melon is a sittings genius. At one time Wendy Newman of Prada was the shoe editor of *Harper's Bazaar*. She told me that she used to get an upset stomach when the shoe issues of *Vogue* came out. I didn't tell her that in the more than 25 years when I went on my own sittings I had stage fright every time. I slept badly the night before, was restless and a little apprehensive. Even today I still have nerves before I show my run-through for a new season. I'm afraid the new styles won't be good enough, that I will lose my cool, say too much or too little, not present it as well as it deserves, fail to put over my point of view. It's important that I keep the vitality in the story, that it does not get watered down or diluted from the original concept and yet I must be receptive to the input of those around me.

When I started my job in 1951 we were lucky to have a few shoes in the offices. The others were either bought or borrowed from a department or specialty store. The stores seldom, if ever, had the shoes in stock as early as we needed them for our press dates, so the number of styles that appeared in each issue was minuscule. I like working in a specialized market like shoes, but I was not interested in working in a market that was an also ran, or an afterthought. It was necessary that I figure out a way to make my markets more significant. Shoe manufacturers complained that the magazines showed so few shoes; therefore, I had meetings with the most important companies to ask them if they would be willing to make new styles in model sizes for our use. For example, the spring shoes that I order in Bologna in September must be made in sizes 8-9-10-11, go through the tedious clearance of customs and be in my office by October 15th. This is difficult because the factories are closed in September and expensive shoes are required to stay on their lasts for a given period of time.

Italy manufactures the finest shoes in the world. Other good quality shoes come from Spain, Brazil and the Orient.

The entire procedure is almost impossible, but at any given time we have approximately 1000 pairs of new shoe styles in sizes and about 200 boots (for autumn) in the *Vogue* fashion closet. They change constantly. Even so we don't always have everything we need in the right color, size, or heel height. The fact that I have stayed in my job more than 35 years is a tribute to my stupidity. When I started in 1951 the average shoe size was 7½. Today it is 9½. We have an increasing number of models with sizes 10½ - 11.

Shoes for *Vogue* must be seen, ordered, made-up and usually photographed before the clothes for the same season are shown. I work with the most outstanding clothes designers before they complete their lines, but even so my job is filled with anxiety, pressure, and very little appreciation. Only a fool would attempt to do it. You have to be a little *mental*, slightly deranged, totally lacking in ego. You must have broad shoulders, a feeble mind, a strong will, thick skin and a consistent record of success in order to have the courage to stick your neck out each season. Fashion is like the theater; you are only as good as your last performance. *Vogue* is kept by the reader for an average of five years, so mistakes must not be made in judgement, interpretation or presentation or they will haunt you for years to come.

My average work day begins at 9:30 a.m. on the dot. By this time I have walked my dog, had my coffee, made notes and am waiting for my assistant to phone me at my apartment. In earlier years I went to the office first thing in the morning, but experience taught me that this was wasted time spent in traffic. Kady, my assistant and I talk at least forty-five minutes. We go over correspondence, phone messages, cables, meet for sittings, requests for market coverage, conferences. I find dictation over the phone more efficient and accurate.

After we finish our morning check-in I go off to my first appointment. Usually I cover two or more designers, time permitting, lunch in an interesting restaurant with business associates, more calls, then back to my Beekman Place apartment, and another lengthy check-in with my office. On days when I have editorial meetings, other meetings or conferences, work in the art department looking at pictures and layouts or copywriters, I go to the office. Always I spend at least one full day and part of other days in my office at 350 Madison Avenue. I would prefer more time in the office but since each picture needs a shoe as well as my own pages, the market consumes my time.

A necessary part of my job is to cover new or potential markets and evaluate their future relationship with *Vogue*. After such a trip to Japan in 1984 I wrote this report:

Japan Trip

"During the long thirteen hour plane trip from New York to Japan my feelings were mixed. I was nervous and apprehensive about the country, about the Japanese people and their culture. I wasn't quite sure what was meant by their culture, or if I would have the sensitivity and intelligence to find out. I had done my homework but I am not blessed with patience and it is a little like walking on eggs. What a fool I must be to take this trip alone.

"I remember how difficult it had been to get someone to speak with me on the phone from the Japanese Trade Commission. Kady had tried to find the right person, with no success. I then contacted Ruder & Finn who represent them. They arranged for a man from the Trade Center to discuss the dates of the Japan Shoe Show with me. He came to the phone but continually interrupted me when I tried to speak. It was not until later that I was told that some Japanese men felt it beneath them to speak with a woman on the phone. They prefer to meet in person so they can see the expression on the woman's face.

"As I thought about the cultural differences I remembered the lunch I had at Cote Basque with Keido Imai, the bright, knowledgeable and de-lightful fashion coordinator of Takashimaya. Geoffrey Beene had introduced me to Keiko and I looked forward to seeing at least part of Japan through her eyes. Keiko told me that Takashimaya was doing their big spring promotion on the arts, crafts and patchwork of the Appalachians from the hills of Kentucky. She had not been allowed to attend the important meetings in Kentucky, but was in New York to do the follow-up work. (It is interesting that while we are examining the influence of Japan, Tokyo's largest department store does its 1984 spring promotion on the products of Kentucky.)

"I realized that I had some thinking adjustment to make concerning the changing role of the Japanese woman. My thoughts on the plane were also about a country whose culture was ancient but whose population was more than 50 percent under the age of 30. This contrast to the U.S.A., a new country with more women over 50 than under, was thought provoking. What does it mean? What does it tell us?

"The Japanese are addicted to American ideas and attitudes. They love our music. They are possessed by our rock. (This may be partially due to their large young population.) They are frantic about T-shirts and punk hair styles. The young people are bright and sparkling and eager. The numerous young boys in the hotels are quiet, clean, polite and pleased with their English. Their posture is straight and erect, and their pride in their work shows in their faces. When they deliver breakfast to your room, they repeat the order to you in English and then smile happily because they get orange juice, scrambled eggs and coffee with no mistakes. I was impressed by these young adults.

"One wonders what makes the Japanese tick. There is no simple answer. Japanese values differ from our own and so does their logic. While the Americans' desire may be more for money, the Japanese have a great passion for more space. The only way for total acceptance in Japan is to be born into their tribe. One is told that their exclusionary behavior seems to come from a strong superiority complex. The Japanese are afraid of the outsider. They feel the influence of the foreigner may cause them to lose their own culture. This may change with the younger generation, but in 1980 only 11 percent of the men had any desire to associate with foreigners, and even though 40 percent of the men under 30 feel differently, it is the men over 60 who run the Japanese companies.

"American individualism is frowned upon by the group oriented Japanese. The consent of the group is how decisions are made in business and in politics. How could a country in fifty years go from a feudal system to what it is today? How is it possible for such a small country to become the world's second largest industrial economy in such a short time? Perhaps it is due to a word that is most frequently heard. The word is efficiency. Combine efficiency with a dogmatic dedication (the company is everything and it is usually a life-long employment) and their economic growth can be partially explained.

"The Japanese are workaholics. They are addicted to their work and also to their company. It is believed that this is perhaps due to their insecurity. Not only is there a scarcity of resources in a small space, but the country is susceptible to tidal waves, earthquakes, and other disasters, and yet their unemployment rate is only 2 percent.

"One cannot help but observe how many Japanese smoke. I do not mean smoke, as we know it. I mean really smoke.

"One interesting footnote: Gloria Noda and I were talking about the fact that the Japanese have permanent employment for life. She explained that this was changing, and that firms had a six month trial period when that did not apply and they were using it. Also she said that, yes, there was their fierce devotion to their companies, but that she felt the average employee did not work very hard. Heiki Imai, the woman who represents Geoffrey Beene and his franchises, told me that thirty people are working on his expected April visit. She felt that the actual work could easily be done by two or three people, but they must subdue their individual efforts and do everything by committee. What a waste of human resources and of the individual spirit and the need to expand the mind and reach beyond oneself. What about fresh ideas, creative thoughts and courage in one's work? It's obvious that they can't fail because they will not try for anything that would fail. Gloria said that she is invited to numerous board meetings and conferences. She must sit quietly, until every man has spoken and by then her ideas have been discussed, dismissed or not needed. A group of men could be talking about a subject that interests her, about which she has some knowledge. When she enters the discussion, they immediately change the subject and ask her a token question on skirt lengths or some such outdated fashion question.

"Japanese architecture is strongly influenced by western ideas, and American architecture is affected by the Japanese. The famous architect Arata Isozaki has responded to western ideas from the early 20th century to the Bauhaus. The Japanese architecture may keep the pallid colors with lots of black or white on white, sometimes three shades of grey. The use of light and materials are still Japanese. To this simplicity they have applied western decoration.

"How special it is to find a country of people packed like sardines, and yet to find a gentleness, a reserve, a politeness, a passion, that runs deep, for all things Japanese. They have learned to live together in close, crowded conditions with little or no noise. Their rooms are tranquil and uncluttered and I find myself speaking in a much lowered voice. I do not know how they make it work for them, but there is little doubt that they do. They are an extraordinary people. They seem to absorb (as if by osmosis) the best of other cultures without even slightly sacrificing their own custom. I find it interesting that when you eat in a Japanese restaurant, they tend to be quiet, reserved. There is very little conversation; but when you eat in a Chinese restaurant, the Japanese, as well as everyone else, are gay, laughing and talking together.

"Ginza Street at night is like the Las Vegas Strip, all bright lights, McDonald's, Southern Fried Chicken and pin-ball machine shops are a part of it, and yet I am told one can walk at night with safety and have no fear for himself or his possessions. Tokyo has the densest population in the world.

"As I began to really see the country, the first awakening came with the beauty of the gardens, their groomed tea bushes, their cryptomeria trees, their bamboo groves. The plum trees bloom first, then the peach, and then the cherry blossoms. There is an entire peach tree, in bloom, in the lobby of the Okura Hotel. It rests in a five-sided water garden with three ancient rocks to complete the design. How very pleasing it is to the eye and sentimental for me, because I grew up in Madison, Georgia, an old village filled with gardens and surrounded by peach orchards.

"For more than twenty-five years I have labored lovingly in my Connecticut gardens. I am proud of them and what I have accomplished, and then I saw what the Japanese have created in the smallest of spaces. Even in winter the colors are sometimes moss greens combined with the grey of trees, or a garden of white sand and grey rocks. How much I have to learn about gardens like the compelling beauty of no color. There is so little that is new, and yet it is as though my eyes are becoming adjusted to a new light.

"The cab drivers must really be frustrated Kamikaze pilots. When they raised their already high fares they must have also doubled their daring. They hate having a foreigner in their cab because the foreigner doesn't know where he is going, and most often neither does the driver. The streets are not marked, and the buildings are numbered according to when they were built. A number 12 could be next to 647. This is not only frustrating but one can get lost for hours. Someone described Tokyo as a spider web that changes.

"This trip is a rare and special experience for me, and yet I worry daily that it produce something special for *Vogue*. Already I find it far more difficult than it has been on previous trips to other countries. The appointments are illusive and the doing of business is long and intricate and no one can make a decision. Business men in New York had told me that it often took two years, or more, to get a decision from a Japanese firm. It is different from the ready-to-wear designers. They now know *Vogue* and the New York *Times* and have had direct results from them. With the shoe designers, not only am I an unknown quantity, but so is *Vogue*. It is very reminiscent of my first trip to Italy in 1956.

"Gloria came with me on my first day of work. She wanted to show me the shops that sold shoes. We started with avant garde shops, then larger stores and then she knew small, out of the way streets that had shops that were crowded with young people. By the end of the day we had literally seen hundreds of shoes. They fell into three categories: copies from America, copies from Italy, (both badly done) and bad taste Japanese shoes. I couldn't find even one pair of Japanese shoes to buy that was both original and of good taste. Needless to say, I went to my hotel that night very discouraged, because I felt that it might well be a forerunner of things to come when I started the manufacturers and designers the following day. I kept remembering that Grace had told me that the important thing I might find, was to find nothing of importance for *Vogue* at this time.

"After many days of digging and a great deal of good help from everyone I could enlist to help me, I found about twelve more or less, creative people who are doing shoes. Some are better than others. I brought home a few of their shoes to show at my run-through. At least five of these designers can develop into interesting shoe people. They are just starting to place orders in America, primarily at Bloomingdales, Saks and Barneys, some for autumn delivery, so our timing was right on target. If I return to Japan to work, for a fall season, in the future it should be later in April.

"I saw Joan Glenn in the lobby of my hotel. Several places I went, they had been. Apparently Bloomingdales is sifting the sands trying to get enough merchandise for their Japanese promotion in September.

"Miss Imai had asked me if I would speak with her bosses before I left; therefore, my last call was Takashimaya. We went through the store and I was amazed to find that they had all the best couture from France and Italy, Each designer with his own shop on the second floor. Geoffrey Beene is a franchised line on the third floor. They do not have his couture line, but he is allowed to show it to a large charity every three years. They have just added his men's line to the store.

"It was interesting that we met in a small conference room, smaller than my office. Six, and at times eight, men sat on one side of the room and a translator and I on the other side. We sat in small arm chairs with a long thin table between us. I, by this time of my trip, was quite tired and had planned to be there about twenty minutes. I had been invited for lunch but I needed to pack. They talked about retailing, shoes, designers, everything you could imagine.

"They wanted information about what new shoe shops had opened in New York, the power (their word) of *Vogue*, their interest in Macy's and Saks and more, Each had many questions, so the meeting lasted for one and one-half hours, during which time several courses of different teas were served. The meeting taught me how good it was to meet in a small space. This enclosure kept us near each other so that no one missed a word of the translation and it gave a feeling of togetherness.

"I feel that Japanese shoes will eventually find a place in the American market — at first in a limited way, as far as numbers of styles. Several designers do have a touch and with careful guidance and selection they will have an influence on a certain category of shoes that we do not, and cannot, make. Also I feel that they can ultimately mean something to *Vogue*, in a financial way as well. Neither the fashions nor the financial will happen overnight; however, we are in on the ground floor.

"The appointments were difficult to make this time (and more difficult to find, even by a good driver), but they will not be in the future. Everything went well at each appointment, and we have made a very good start toward a continued working relationship. Our talks together about shoes were especially productive. The people at each appointment were especially pleased that my card was printed in Japanese. This was a compliment to them and the meeting started on a friendly note.

"At one appointment where the shoes were what I call "St. Louis shoes," I found the president of the company to be distinguished and interesting to talk to. He spoke no English, neither did his group of seven who attended the meeting, but he was very knowledgeable. He wanted to know if *Vogue* started in France or America, and when. I said I thought it was 1885 but he quickly remembered it was 1886. As a great compliment to him, he said, a friend had presented him with a book, some years back, by a woman named Chase. The same friend had it translated for him. I thought how delighted Edna Woolman Chase would have been.

"Immediately upon arrival for each appointment, a cup of coffee, not tea, was set before you. The coffee was the supreme compliment to the American. Also, very quickly they are learning English. Some firms at present are having English lesson seminars so that at least a limited group of executives can make contact in English."

(I have eliminated the last page of this report that contained my recommendations concerning Vogue's future relationship with the Japanese Shoe Market.)

I was asked to speak at *Vogue's* yearly sales conference. This is always a difficult task because I don't know what might interest these specialized super salesmen, and I doubt if I will ever find out. Regardless, I must say something, so I decided to talk in part on the woman over 50. On my holiday that summer I had read a journal by May Sarton on her 70th year. She has written more than 30 books, also she has written for *Vogue*. She lives alone on the coast of Maine. Since I know her, I spoke to her on the phone about the book and she explained to me, "I am happier at 70 than I have ever been, and have more power (a strange word from a poet). I know what I want. I am more patient. I have more inner resources and more money than I have had, and oddly, I buy more clothes for my lecture tours. I am more daring, especially about long dresses."

Also, I told about Peggy Hays. I have a friend, Patrick Slavin, a young man of 25 who attended Berkeley. Living near the campus is an 88 year old woman by the name of Peggy Hays. She is the sister of Alexander Calder who lived, until his death, in Roxbury. His wife Louisa still lives in the village. Patrick's mother Maeve was visiting her son in San Francisco. She phoned Peggy to invite her to dinner with the young people to whom she had been a friend. Peggy said that she could not speak at that time. When she came to dinner she explained that she had a 19 year old dog who had lived his time and was being put to sleep by her vet. Her son was there and they had a lovely funeral for the dog in the backyard. Maeve said, "Peggy, you must get a new puppy." This dear lady of almost 90 said, "No, it would just mean in another 19 years I would have to go through the same thing again."

One summer afternoon I went to the small village of Southbury to meet a weekend guest who had come from New York City to spend the weekend in the country. While I waited for the bus, a little old lady drove up in her car with another lady seated beside her. She was so small she had to look through the steering wheel to see the road and she hit the curb when she parked. The driver went into the little shop to get a schedule. By this time the bus had come in and my friend had arrived and was sitting in my car. The two ladies next to us were having words. I was interested and said to my friend that the little lady seemed too old to be driving. As we listened the driver turned to her passenger and said, "But Mother, if you don't change buses in Hartford you will have to change stations in Boston." Mother replied that she did not give a damn, she hated Hartford and had no intention of changing buses there. With that she got out of the car, slammed the door, got on the bus and drove away.

I love the spirit and spunk of such women, and thank God there are many of them.

In order to be good in fashion, one must have more than a normal amount of curiosity, and she should be creative. He or she should be intrigued by his work, so involved in what he is doing that he forgets about the time spent doing it. He should train himself to remember what he has seen. This can be done if he works at it. I do not take a notebook to my appointment. What would I do if I lost it? I think I have a photographic memory. In any event, I have reached the stage where I can see hundreds of shoes in a day and not only remember most, if not all, of them but also who made them.

I tell design student groups to whom I often speak, that they must be aware of everything around them — of all colors, or the lack of color. When I go into a room to lecture I look around quickly (usually everyone is writing proudly in a notebook) then turn my back to the group and ask them if anyone knows if I have on jewelry or if they can tell me the color of my eyes. I tell them how many are male and how many are female. Also I usually describe what at least 12 of them are wearing. Then I turn toward the group and several of them are still writing; however, I was able to get the attention of most of them.

A person good at fashion must be observant, aware, interested, have good taste, and above all remember what he has seen or done. What good is experience if one does not retain? What has been seen I store away for future reference.

To be a success in the field of fashion, a young person must learn not to take criticism personally. That's a big statement and one of the hardest lessons to learn. It is necessary to be sensitive, to be alive to every vibration, and yet not take it too much to heart. The ones who become too emotionally and personally offended seem to burn out before they have learned all that is needed to excel at their chosen profession.

There are too many young people waiting for every good job, so learning well is important. I tell students to listen, learn, absorb like a sponge, feel involved, but wait to be asked for an opinion. Too often youthful enthusiasm takes over and an uninformed beginner speaks out before he has anything significant to offer. Be prepared with knowledge. You'll be asked; your time will come.

Every editor worth her salt has a group of young talented people in the business who are special to her. She watches, encourages, lends a hand, delights in the growth of their careers. It's one of the pure glittering joys of her work, to follow a motivated young talent as he or she matures and makes a significant contribution to his chosen profession.

Through the large number of years that I have been at *Vogue* I've seen a good number stretch and reach beyond their supposed limits. They have a common denominator. Each is hungry to succeed, has an overactive imagination, tireless energy and the ability to carefully choose whose advice he takes. He also allows himself to make mistakes, bounce back and most important of all, not to believe his own press notices.

I have three examples of the above. Maya Bowler is an English designer for Impo and has a line in the works under her own name. She has a young son whose name is Hays, something that pleases me.

Maya came to my office some years ago, with two large shoe cases that were filled with samples of her first American line. I liked the line, I liked her sparkle, enthusiasm and spirit, so I asked if she could leave me eight samples for possible use in *Vogue*. We offered to have a messenger return her oversized cases back to her hotel, the Algonquin. The messenger lost the cases and poor Maya's first line was gone. I felt terrible and so did *Vogue*. We asked if she could stay in New York an extra week so we could try to make everything right.

Luckily I had kept the eight shoes. Maya draws well and we liked the designs so we asked her to do a drawing of each one for use in *Vogue*. We paid for this, as well as her hotel bill and the insurance settled with her manufacturer.

I invited Maya to go to my mill for the weekend. She was young, filled with energy and turned out to be a natural born gardener, for she had grown up in the country. Instead of crying into her beer, she became a charming helpful guest and endeared herself to me from that day forward. I introduced her to the president of I. Miller, and he sent her to Jerry Miller. Together Maya and Jerry had a rewarding and lucrative association designing and manufacturing shoes in Greece.

I've known Sam Edelman since before he was born, on my birthday. He is tall, lean, appealing and smart, perhaps too much a workaholic for his own good, but a big success managing and directing the Esprit line of shoes. He and his wife Libby live near San Francisco with their two adopted children. I get a kick out of following their climb to fame.

Geoffrey Kalinsky is a very young man with a big growth potential. He runs the office and sales for Pupi d'Angiepi. Pupi manufactures their own shoes, as well as those of Donna Karan and Ferdi. Geoffrey is so bright he sparkles. He is cute, huggable, thrilled with life and he works and dresses in a charming individualistic way. He makes me feel good to be in his presence, and he deserves my help and attention in *Vogue*. His father, a retailer in Charleston, S.C. must be proud of his beautiful son. I am.

It is not unusual to spend three evenings each week on business in a good restaurant. Because my day is tiring and must be productive, I insist on having an early dinner. This allows me time with myself and my dog. A pad is kept beside my bed and I jot down thoughts for the next day as well as follow through from the dinner discussions. No two days are similar but the time segments are more or less the same. The biggest amount of time is spent in lines, cars, cabs, gridlock and planes.

I usually serve on two, no more than three, boards and work with at least one commission such as mental health, drugs or education. Not that it is expected of me, but because I believe in doing so, and it broadens my scope. It helps me.

It is not unusual for an editor to be seated next to a total stranger at a banquet or dinner. There are times when something must be done to break the ice so that the evening will not seem like a week. Jessica Daves told me there are three subjects that always work:

1. How nice to hear your good news.
2. Tell me about yourself.
3. Is it true what they say about you?

In 1959 I made a trip, for *Vogue*, to all the Scandinavian countries. The Fine Arts Society of each country acted as my host and introduced me to their creative people. I had not been in Finland many hours before I realized Armi Ratia was the power behind the creative forces in her country. She was also quite a woman — warm, tender, strong, demanding, brilliant, overly endowed with a refreshing sense of humor, and above all a person who gets things done by inspiring those around her.

I fell in love with Finland, and a number of visits since have kept the love affair alive. I owe it all to Armi, since I saw the country through her eyes. The first few days that we spent together were unforgettable since neither of us understood what the other was saying. She speaks English, and six other languages which she sprinkles through her conversation without knowing it.

We were both propelled by the creative search and found it easy to communicate through design. Herrings, aquavit, vodka, salmon, sour cream, large lakes, great creative design — tapestries, wooden furniture, crafted rugs and Marimekko are the first things one thinks of when one thinks of Finland. When I think of Finland the first thing that comes to mind is Armi. She taught me how much the Finns love music, drama, dancing, sun, daylight. They play hard and they work hard. They live for the midsummer festival on the longest day of the year, around the middle of June, when the weather is usually excellent. Armi says they long for this sunlight and gaiety, but if they blink they miss the whole thing. Good weather lasts such a short period of time, and they have come through a long dark winter when the light lasts only a few brief hours.

Armi Ratia was the owner and founder of Marimekko. She was born in Darelia, close to the Russian frontier. In 1951 she founded Marimekko.

This small Finnish company has had a marked influence upon printed fabrics over the world. Eugenia Sheppard, in her column in the *New York Post*, November 13, 1963, called Marimekko a "Uniform for intellectuals."

Armi has her own thoughts of what Marimekko means:

> "I really don't sell the clothes, I sell a way of living. They are designs, not fashions... Cutting is as simple as possible. My approach is something like the architect's. He makes a house for people to live in; I make a dress for women to live in.
>
> "They are for the woman who wants to forget her dress. They are for such women as the many intellectuals we have in Finland ... who do not have to make such a fuss about what they put on."

My second trip to Finland was in August 1965. I went along with Gordon Parks, who photographed a six-page story on Marimekko for *Vogue*. This feature appeared in the November 15 issue the same year.

Armi had four rooms in four different places prepared for me: A suite in the Hotel Marski, a large room in her country house on the sea, a room in her town house in Helsinki, and a complete office set up at the Marimekko factory. The bedrooms were delightfully done with printed sheets, Marimekko hand printed fabrics, a record player (all Russian music), and even an American typewriter. Each morning when we came to the factory a new dress for me to wear was hanging in my office.

In the evenings at Bokars, her country estate, which I preferred after spending the day in Helsinki, she would announce to her numerous guests — the large house and six smaller houses on the estate were always filled with guests — "Tonight we dress long." When we came back from the sauna a long dress, the right size, was hanging in every room.

One of the red cottages was a store house filled with clothes for the use of her visitors. She also had proper attire for the men. In each guest room there was also a sauna robe made of printed terry cloth.

The evening meal was perfection and always rather formal until the vodka began flowing. Cocktails before dinner are frowned upon by the Finns. They do most of their drinking with the meal and afterward.

The story that I was doing on Marimekko started with the design. These designs were then printed on cotton, terry-cloth, or wool. The designers made the patterns for the clothes, we even had boots made from the large plaid blankets. When everything was complete, we flew to Finnish Lapland, just twenty miles below the Arctic Sea, and Gordon photographed them in the wild, beautiful location.

I found the work hard, with the language barrier, and at three o'clock one afternoon asked Armi if we could just have an informal dinner together without the guests to discuss our plans. This was a challenge for her. I think she realized she had given me too little quiet attention and that even though she enjoyed watching me bring the job together, she had been working me too hard and this was a chance to set it right. She called in a dozen assistants and hurriedly gave them instructions in Finnish. We left the factory at 5:30 p.m., just the two of us with Armi driving which was a mistake because her pride prevents her from wearing glasses. Enroute to the country we passed a battalion of military soldiers marching on a narrow bridge we had to cross. After we passed she said, "Was there someone along the road?" As she speeded along she kept saying, "It isn't really this far."

Two of her cars followed us with costumes, but I was not sure then why. When we reached Bokars she suggested that I go to sauna, then have a nap before dinner at seven, and please dress Hungarian. I did my best, along with clothes that were brought to my room, to look Hungarian. When I appeared for dinner I found she and I were dining alone in the upstairs music room. Armi came in fabulously dressed, and we sat down at the table decorated with a Hungarian flavor. We ate Hungarian food which was delicious, especially with a Finnish touch, and then dancers appeared up the stairs, in costume, to entertain us. Armi had persuaded four groups of dancers that had just closed at the opera house in Helsinki to come to Bokars and perform for just the two of us. She adored the drama and I was enchanted by the scene.

I liked the printed sheets that were on my numerous beds; so I asked if special prints could be made for each bed in my New York apartment and my country house. My sheets were printed and made in Finland. Now Marimekko sheets are made in the United States. Since 1966 I have used these sheets on my bed in Roxbury, and even though they have always been washed commercially, they seem not to have faded or lost much of the color.

The third time I went to Finland was on the inaugural flight of FinnAir from New York to Helsinki.

English *Vogue* went to Finland in 1969 to do a feature on Marimekko and cold weather fashions. They asked Armi to write a feature on Finland. I would like to share it with you:

> "Cry is My Message, Laugh is My Weapon. I tried to get a telephone call to Helsinki from New York.
>
> "Operator, please give me Helsinki, Finland."
>
> "What — where is that?"
>
> "Finland — that is the country. Finland. FINLAND. F-I-N-L-A-N-D. It is between Russia and Sweden..."
>
> "Oh, Sweden, of course..."
>
> "NOT Sweden. Finland..."
>
> "...I got my call finally, but learned again how small and how little known a country Finland is, even if it covers a larger area than England, Scotland and Ireland together.
>
> "The map of Finland looks like a female figure. The lady has Russia on the east and Sweden on the west. Her skirt is in the Gulf of Finland, and her head touches the Arctic Ocean. That gives quite a good picture of Finland's geographical and political position — and her economic position, too.

"Finland was part of the Swedish empire for about 650 years, from the middle of the 12th century until 1809. The Czar Alexander I made Finland an autonomous Grand Duchy.

"Now she has been independent for fifty years. How is it possible, after all those phases in history, after forty-two wars with Russia — all lost — and after the powerful influence of Sweden in our culture, religion and economy, that we are still Finns and Finland?

"In fact, during the centuries we have grown independent in the real sense of the word. We came to this country not as a subordinate horde of soldiers or as pilgrims. We came towards new forests as individuals, hunters, and fishermen, and it took time before we started agriculture and even longer — fifty years longer than others in Europe — to start industry. That might partially explain our fierce sense of freedom.

"We seem capable of feeling free. It may be innocence or ignorance or simply survival, but I have a feeling that we also want to put values in such order that power, money or suffering do not reach us. We Finns are considered to be rough, boring, silent, slow. But perhaps too many foreign promises have proved empty.

"The first Englishman who came here we killed before he had time to explain the reason for his visit. He was Bishop Henry who only wanted to give us pagans the blessing of Christendom. Since then we have had a much more practical and polite relationship. Britain is our biggest buyer of paper, pulp and timber.

"On closer contact you will find a Finn to be a most faithful friend. The Finns have a sense of humor, too, but it is difficult to cross the language barrier.

"And their slowness can be deceiving. When you see Finns in winter in heavy dark coats, boots and fur hats, awkwardly moving like bundles on the streets you cannot mistake them for French or Italian. But when the precious sun comes, it floats into their veins and you can see them dance and dance in the open air and on the jetties. Music means much to the Finns, being one of the channels for their feelings and one of their talents.

"They say that Sibelius might have never become so well known if his *Valse Triste* had not suddenly been played in every cafe in Paris. Now Sibelius is famous for his symphonies and no Finn can listen to *Finlandia* without pride. In fact, *Finlandia* tells so much of Finland that you see the lacework of lakes (more than half of our country is covered by water), you see our hills, green lovely slopes in Karelia, endless swamps with fierce colours and the pointed fir trees, sad but lush, and the virginal birch trees standing white. After the ice age, granite — the reddish groundrock, old as the Himalayas — was violently thrown over Finland. You can see those rocks in surprising places, looking like the aftermath of a giant's ball game. Napoleon's grave in Paris is made from Finnish granite.

"In the arts, architecture must come first. Professor Alvar Aalto's famous diagonal stroke and his individual genius is unquestionable. He still creates today and his sarcasm is still biting elegantly. Small Aaltos around the world are as many as Corbusiers or Mies van de Rohes. We lost a fine architect and fine person in Viljo Revell, whose Toronto Town Hall is the pride of Canada. Then there is Professor Aarno Ruusuvuori, who as a teacher has given aesthetic tools to generations of architects and is leaving a lasting mark in Helsinki. Some churches and factory buildings also show his master hand. There are others — Heikki Siren, Aarne Ervi, Riema Peitila...and many young ones coming.

"One thing that all foreigners notice is women working in the fields. You also see women working beside men on buildings and even repairing roads. You meet them as uniformed bus drivers, tram drivers, post women and working in petrol stations. Almost all our dentists are women, and many are doctors, architects, engineers. Women take part in politics and social organizations, but although quite common in middle management, they are rare in high business positions.

"The sauna, when taken correctly and not with all the frightening aspects of bad commercial fakes — suffocating heat, hot waves and bruising 'vasta' made of birch — becomes a mental as well as physical passion. In a real sauna you just feel the luxury of warmth, water and total cleanliness. The sauna John Cowan photographed on page 108 is my own in the end of a long jetty, a former boathouse, where old Jussi built one of the best saunas in Finland, air circulating perfectly, two windows giving a view of land and sea and the biggest swimming pool of all, the Gulf of Finland. In winter there is a hole in the thick ice and I dip in it and have not died.

"Finnish cooking is mainly Russian and heavy. There is too much fat in it and it is one of the main causes of illness. But the crayfish — they are a

101

chapter on their own. These baby lobsters are the reason for a row of parties beginning in July and only ending when even the most passionate crayfish eaters find the scale too hard. Quite a lot of vodka belongs to the ritual. The Finns drink. Yes, they do, but no more than other northern countries and only half what Americans consume a year.

"What is it like to live in Finland? Finns travel a lot, and they could easily get work in other countries, being considered an honest, hard-working and quite capable people. But — as an American told me — Finnish girls are good only until they get that dreamy look and begin to speak about midsummer in Finland and the Kaki — the cuckoo bird — and their homesickness becomes bigger than dollars, pounds and francs. That is true. We Finns voluntarily live in this cold, expensive, demanding hard country of ours. We may rebel and we criticize the government, the system, the stupid leaders as in every other country, but don't you dare to come and tell that to us, YOU. We want to solve the same problems as other people today all over the globe in our own obstinate, free, persistent way. We have to find our liberation as human beings with senses sharpened to the dangers of a small country, where isolation may feel depressing and the limits too overpowering. Our young people are very healthy and strong. We have a beautiful country to put on the map of the world and we will do it. With science, with innovation, with talent, with courage.

"There are people who say that Finns only get out from their self-conscious shell by drinking or by acting. That's why we have so many theaters, at least one in every bigger town and hundreds of

102

amateur theatres. Shakespeare is the most popular writer — 871 performances during that last ten years — next come Moliere', Chekov and Shaw.

"Isn't it strange that in a language which only 4.8 million stubborn people speak, more literature is published per person than anywhere else in the whole world? The Finns read. In 1686 the wise Bishop Gezelius demanded that all who wished to get married should learn Luther's Small Catechism. So only people able to read could get married... So even the dullest of boys and girls in Finland can read.

"In Finnish literature, Aleksis Kivi is the name. His *Seven Brothers* reflects Finnish characteristics so well that once an American diplomat looked around at a cocktail party and found all those seven characters present: Juhani, Simeoni, Aapo, Timo, Lauri, Toumas and Eero. And then we have our national epic, Kalevala, and miles of national poetry where all the ancient wisdom is collected. Modern Finnish literature loses so much in translation. But that happens in every language.

"Finnish is extremely difficult to learn. With its many singing vowels it reminds one of some southern tropical island: Jo valkene kaukainen ranta ja kiollisesti aurinko nousee... Hard to believe but you could find a Finnish work with one consonant and seven vowels: haayoaie, which means 'intention to spend a wedding night.'

"After *Vogue*'s fashion team worked through minus 25 degrees centigrade here, John Huston came with a crew of 120 people to film 'The Kremlin Letter' which takes place partly in Moscow. This is the third time Helsinki and Finland have had the honor to act as Russia. First came *Doctor Zhivago* then *Billion Dollar Brain*, and now Richard Boone, Patrick O'Neal and Barbara Perkins wade in three yards of snow and minus 20 degrees centigrade with their *Kremlin Letter* around Helsinki. I only hope they do not get the idea of making a film from Helsinki in Moscow, since we still consider we are part of western civilization in spite of strong strokes of the east in our mental make-up.

"'How do you personally feel that borderline of east and west, Mrs. Ratia?' I was asked in London. Well, the western in me is more rational, the eastern more calmly calculating and cruel. The western is more composed, conscious and alert, the eastern letting go, sentimental, fierce in joy and sorrow. As a Finn, cry is my message, laugh is my weapon."

Gordon Parks arrived in Finland two weeks after I came. Everything was ready for his pictures. We chose Ristomatti Ratia, Armi's first son, to act as Gordon's assistant. They got along beautifully. We took pictures at Bokars, and in Helsinki and were scheduled to fly to Finnish Lapland to complete the assignment. On the day set aside for our flight we found that we were behind schedule, due to weather conditions. Shooting was going well at flight time and Gordon casually said, "What a shame, to leave this superb light." Armi left us for a few minutes, phoned someone she knew at FinnAir and requested a plane to take the party of eight, three hours later. When she returned she explained that the plane would be ready but we must take our own food. We boarded with cases of wine and enormous baskets of food prepared by Armi's kitchen staff. The pilot and hostesses were delightful. They told us about the country as we flew northward. When we reached the most northern airport, we took cars for the rest of the trip.

Awaiting in my room at the small hotel where we stayed were two dozen red roses along with Marimekko candles, sheets, tablecloths for meals, and a telegram that said, "Welcome at last to Lapland. Love, Armi."

I was flabbergasted by it all. Imagine all this waiting in a small hotel just under the Arctic Sea. I asked how it got there. Armi smiled, pleased that she had pulled it off, and said, "Oh, it was flown up yesterday."

Vogue prepared a promotional piece of the six Marimekko pages that we published in the magazine. Marimekko mailed 100,000. I spoke of Lapland in an article I wrote for the mailing.

> "The photographs on these six pages were made against the sea and the weird settings of Lapland, photographed just slightly eighty miles below the Arctic Sea. Finland is shaped like a lady. These pictures were made about the center of her head in a special area called Kaunispa (means beautiful head). This is an area where the informed go for walking tours and skiing. Reindeer are frequently seen. We were there at the time of year when they acquire the rich, lush fur coats for the winter that follows. During these long months no daylight is seen and the Lapps are confined to their own families. The dark period is called Kaamos. It lasts from October to after December. Because of the deep snows and weather conditions, a fever called Lapland fever attacks one here, another there — without warning. It is a sort of insanity that sometimes comes from the darkness, the remoteness when one feels he must get to the sun, to warmth, to people.
>
> "A man may leave his home without warning and head on foot toward the south. Naturally he must be brought back to save his life from the winter harshness...

"Lapland is lushly spooky, almost hypnotic in its wildness. It draws one magnetically to climb higher and to walk even beyond one's own strength. A hiker may go out for three hours, return eight or ten hours later. For the seeing eye and the aware, Finnish Lapland quietly, secretly slips up on one; it intoxicates long before you realize you have drunk of its hidden beauty. This is no place for those who seek the obvious or those who lack the eye for searching. It is all there, but elusive, unless one gets caught up in the mood of the land. Upon leaving, one keeps looking over one's shoulder, for Lapland seems to follow like a shadow.

"We were lucky to get four rooms at this small hotel in Lapland, so we gave one to the two models, one to Gordon, who needed extra space for his equipment, one to Vee and Risto, Armi's husband and son, and she and I shared a room.

"Armi had reserved the sauna for Saturday evening. This was the only way to get a bath. As we met other people in the halls she invited them to join us at the sauna. The men shared sauna at one time and the women another. I am no prude but it seemed strange to share a sauna with twenty women I had never met! Armi explained that in a small place like this it was the polite thing to do.

"The models and Risto had eaten something not quite right during the day, and all three were quite sick. We had taken them to the only doctor in the region, and he put them to bed with medication. This put a damper on the Saturday night gaiety. It did not restrain the Lapps' happiness; there was a sign posted on the entrance wall that said, 'Tonight we dance.' And they danced without shedding their heavy boots or parkas.

106

"After sauna Gordon and Vee went to the living room and had a supper with brandy before the fire. Armi and I went to our room. It was a narrow sparse room with two small cots. If we both decided to get out of bed at the same time we would have had a collision. We drank a bottle of good champagne brought from Bokars and ate Welsh rarebit. By the time I returned from the ladies room, Armi was snoring loudly. It seemed silly to retire so early, especially since it was light outside and continued to be light all night; so I put on a robe and joined Vee and Gordon at the fireplace.

"It was necessary to walk through the dancing Lapps to get to the so-called living room. Armi is fond of the brandy bottle, so they assumed I had left her drunk. In about fifteen minutes she appeared, cold sober, saying, 'That goddam Lapp tried to rape me.' When we uncovered the true facts, they were something like this: When I left our room I had not completely closed one of the double doors to our room, and the wind had blown both doors open. There lay Armi, in the raw since she sleeps that way. Candles were burning on the shelf behind the beds; so I guess the Lapp took this candle lighted scene as an invitation. When he crawled into her bed she screamed, 'Get the hell out of this room.' Risto heard her from the next room and naturally assumed she was speaking to me. He went to the models and said they might as well prepare to leave Lapland since Armi was screaming at Kay.

"Armi said she told the Lapp, who roomed directly across the hall, that I would soon return from the ladies room. He knew that I was with Vee and Gordon and said so.

"It was decided that Vee would visit our neighbors across the hall and speak to them. While he was doing this I asked why she hadn't let the Lapp stay and she explained that he was too small."

Vee and Armi had thirty-five explosive years before they finally got a divorce. They have three children: Ristomatti, Antimatti, and Errica. All three have worked at Marimekko.

I may as well tell another story on Armi; she would find it amusing that I remembered. I had picked her up at a New York hotel, where she seldom stays these days. On the drive to Roxbury she told me that she had had a gigolo. The night before, a friend and I had stopped by to have a nightcap with her after the theater. Armi asked Joe, "How much does a call girl get in this hotel?" He explained that the hour made the difference.

As she told me about her gigolo I understood why she asked. She had a suite with two bedrooms. Risto and his wife Kerstin, who was very pregnant, shared one bedroom; there was a living room between their room and their mother's bedroom.

Armi told me that she ordered white wine. (I had tried to get her to drink white wine instead of brandy since she already had cirrhosis of the liver, and later died from it. She left me in her will my choice of her works of art by the famous ceramic artist Kaipianen.) The same man, an assistant manager, brought the wine to her suite. One night he came, opened the wine and they drank it together. He then very carefully closed the second door to the bedroom; they retired to her room and got into bed. She had recently had plastic surgery on her bosoms, so I asked her what she did about it. She said, "Do not touch." After a brief time in bed the man said, "You f--- like a rabbit. I thought you were a cosmopolitan woman of the world." I asked her what she said and she replied, "I gave him fifty dollars. Was that enough?"

I told her that it seemed unwise to have gone to bed with someone from the hotel, that the story would get around. Armi said, "But think what good room service I'll get."

On one of Armi's visits to New York we were at dinner with a group of business associates. Someone asked if Marimekko was doing well. Armi told a story on herself. Part of her charm was her humor and her ability to tell all. She had a habit of signing her cables with the word love, even when they were strictly business matters. The company hired a new director and he set about to cut down all unnecessary expenses. One of the first things he did was to remove the word love from the cables, explaining that this would save a goodly amount of Finnish marks. All seemed to be going well until it was noted little by little that business was on a slow downward curve. At the time when stores visited Finland for market week Armi asked several of her retail friends from Africa, Australia, and Italy for lunch. She explained that she was proud of Marimekko's present line and wondered why their foreign retail sales were sliding downward. The store owner from Africa explained that they felt she no longer cared about them because love had been omitted from her cables. Soon afterward the new director called a special board meeting and decreed that from this day forward love will be reinstated in all cables.

On her fourteenth birthday Armi wrote these three lines in a notebook she kept:

"There in only one responsibility — beauty.
There is only one reality — a dream.
There is only one strength — love."

Wanda Ferragamo is a fabulous woman. When I was in Florence one March, Wanda and her chauffeur picked me up at the Excelsior early on a Saturday morning. We drove into the country to an antiques fair; both of us adore antiques. Then on to one of her country homes. It is a large white Normandy style house. Fiamma, her daughter, and her husband met us there, as well as several guests.

At this farm Wanda has a winery and she took great delight in showing me how it worked. Also there was a small chapel at the farm. We had a delicious meal, served by a waiter in white gloves, good wine and conversation. Following the meal, she made crepes over the fire from a patterned crepe maker with long iron handles. It was a copy of an early 400 B.C. model. Both the early 400 B.C. model and the copy were a gift to me. The old one for my dining room wall, along with the other antique cooking utensils that hang there, and the copy to use for making crepes over my own fireplaces.

When Wanda was in Roxbury, Maeve Slavin wrote an article about her for the *New Milford Times* Magazine called "Preview." It is well-written and filled with details, and I will share it with you:

"'I consider our life in Florence like an island, with nice strong bridges all over the world. We don't interfere in politics. Our time is devoted to the work. We don't know a lot of what is going on; we are so happy with our work. A big island, with the bridges, that is the truth.'

"Speaking was Wanda Ferragamo, wife of the great Italian shoemaker, who died in 1960. A woman of warmth, charm, intelligence, humor, kindness, and an indominatable will, she was spending a heavy business trip in the United States.

"However, relaxation is not something that Mrs. Ferragamo adapts to easily. The weekend was taken up with a relentless round of antique shops, sight-seeing, and meeting old friends and new. Her keen eye missed nothing from maple syrup to presents for her eleven grandchildren — and the twelfth expected in August.

"'This woman rules an empire,' said her hostess, Kathryne Hays, a *Vogue* magazine editor.

"Indeed she does. When Salvatore Ferragamo died in 1960 he left in her care not only six children, the oldest of whom was 17, but an empire and also a dream. The empire was based on the Ferragamo internationally acclaimed shoe, an object of elegance, quality, craftsmanship, and comfort. Salvatore Ferragamo believed in healthy

110

feet, and devoted his inspiration to devising shoes that enhanced the health as well as the look of a foot.

"The dream was the expansion of the Ferragamo philosophy to include everything a woman needs to be both fashionable and at ease: Dresses, shirts, sweaters, scarves, bags.

"'My husband dreamed that one day a woman could walk into a Ferragamo shop and walk out with everything beautiful, everything nice. And it's happening now,' Mrs. Ferragamo said with some pride.

"Salvatore Ferragamo also believed in the importance of the family, as does his widow. The children would be the ones to make the dream come true.

"'The year before he died, my husband felt something. He knew he would not live much longer. He asked me to persuade our oldest daughter, Fiamma, to leave her studies and come to work near his desk, so that she could learn what he had to teach her. She didn't want to do it, but now she is very glad.'

"Fiamma, then 33, married to the Marchese de San Guliano, has two children and expects a third this summer. She is in charge of the design of shoes, bags and luggage.

"Next is Giovanna, who accompanied her mother on the trip. She is a lovely, shy young woman, married to a mechanical engineer, and the mother of four children. Giovanna was 15 when she began work with her father. She designs all the clothes under the Ferragamo name, and also the fabrics. Coordinated shirts and sweaters are a major part of the Ferragamo style image, and this involves designing silk and cotton fabrics, and

111

matching them to wool for sweaters, jackets and skirts. The clothes are coordinated with the shoe styles and colors, so that the complete Ferragamo line is consistent.

"Giovanna said that when she began designing clothes her father told her that he was lending her enough money to get the project started. It was up to her to make it a success in every way, and repay the loan.

"'I was more frightened that I could not repay my father than of anything else,' she said.

"Now she prepares nine collections a year, for worldwide distribution — men's shirts and sweaters as well as women's clothes — and runs a large household. Her eldest child is eleven, and her youngest is one year old. The eleven year old is already running the family chicken farm ('twelve chickens') and making it pay by selling the produce to his mother. 'That way he will learn,' she says.

"Ferruchio, the eldest son, is vice president and general manager of the company. He is married to an English wife, and they have three children, identical twin boys, four years old, and each named for a grandfather, Salvatore and James, and a little girl, the apple of her grandmother's eye.

"Fulvia is married to a lawyer and lives in Milan. She coordinates Giovanna's fabric designs with factory production.

"Leonardo, who is 23, is in charge of the technical part of the business. And the only reason that the sixth child Massimo, is not involved is that he is 18 years old and still at school. 'He will be our lawyer,' his mother says firmly. 'He is so kind and sweet that all our American friends say he should be in charge of promotion. They call him our Kissinger, always diplomatic, always nice. But he will be the lawyer.'

"When Wanda Miletti married Salvatore Ferragamo she was 16 and he 42. The eleventh child of a poor family, he had started work as a cobbler when he was nine years old, and when he was 14 he emigrated to America where he had been told the shoes were beautiful and miraculous.

"'Recently when I was going through some papers,' Mrs. Ferragamo said, 'I found his first passport. I felt so much emotion, I cannot describe it to you.'

"Young Salvatore was successful in America, with a shop in Santa Barbara and commissions to design for the movies in Hollywood. He had specialized in the custom-made shoe, but he reached a point where he realized that he would have to go to machine production to keep pace with his orders. He searched all over the United States but couldn't find a factory that met his stringent requirements to quality. So, in 1927 he returned to Italy and in Florence found the crafts-manship and sensitivity he was looking for. Until 1933 the Ferragamo shoes, made in Florence and sold in America, carried the 35 year old tycoon to fame and fortune. But the Depression brought disaster, and in 1933 he was bankrupt.

"'He had three lire,' Mrs. Ferragamo said, 'With three loyal craftsmen working in the court-yard of his house he began again.'

"While still an undischarged bankrupt, he was able to buy his headquarters the Palazzo Feroni-Spini, completed in 1289, overlooking the Ponte Santa Trinita on the Arno River. The same year, 1938, he bought 'Il Palagio,' a villa in Fiesole, overlooking Florence, which Michelangelo is said to have remodeled from a village fortress, as the summer home of the Strozzi family. That same year he was discharged from bankruptcy, and was a multi-millionaire and world famous.

"So, at the age of 42, he felt it was time to find a wife. He travelled all over Italy on this romantic quest, and finally in his home village, Bonito, outside Naples, he found the girl he was seeking, the daughter of the Mayor and family doctor. And they lived happily ever after.

"Wanda Ferragamo had spent her married life taking care of the children and the household. She says she learned to speak English because she heard her husband talking to American visitors about 'my wife' and she wanted to know what he was saying. 'So I asked an English lady, who had been the companion of a neighbor of ours, to come and teach me English every afternoon for two hours.'

"When her husband died, she was still a young woman, not yet forty, but she was completely inexperienced in business. She has remedied this situation as efficiently as she mastered the English language.

"'It was good for me. When I was working, I didn't miss him. I thought he was away on a business trip. When I went home in the evening it all came back to me, but the children were all still at home, and I had to face the problems of the household, somebody's school, somebody sick. A friend said to me, 'Don't you think about your husband?' And I replied, 'My dear, I have no time to think.'

"Today, with all but the two youngest married, Wanda Ferragamo manages not only the business, as President of the company, but also three homes, the Fiesole property, a farm in the mountains at Cortina, and a house in Capri. All the married children have houses on the properties, and the family ties are strong.

"'But,' she added, 'I say this not from the money point of view. This work keeps us together, keeps us communicating. It is like a privilege.'

"'And,' she added, ' please, say this too. Our work is a function of love. Everywhere I go I look for love. And I found it here, here in America, here in this house: Love, and flowers, and color. It is very, very nice.'"

It was a crisp, chilly, sunny Sunday morning in March of this year, 1976, when I left Florence. Mrs. Ferragamo sent her Mercedes and chauffeur to drive me to Bologna.

Before we left I had a call from Mandy, Ferruchio's English wife, asking that I wait at the hotel until they arrived. Soon after I looked up and saw coming through the revolving doors of the Excelsior, Mandy, tall and striking in her long-haired fur coat, with a darling little boy holding each of her hands. She was followed by Ferruchio, who looks like a prince, holding the hand of his young daughter. Their enormous dog followed close behind. It was a sight to behold.

I told this story to Wanda and she said, "They would have brought the pony if you had asked them to do so."

Today, October 5, 1976, I had lunch at Orsini's with Helen O'Hagan, the very capable and attractive vice president and special events director of Saks Fifth Avenue, and Leonardo Ferragamo, the second from the youngest son. We were discussing Florence and Leonardo asked me if I knew the story of the pony. He said that his mother, Wanda, had been in Ischia and had seen the pony with its cart in the village square. The children were having rides. She spoke to

115

the owner and said, "I must have the pony and the cart for my grandchildren." He sold her the pony and cart, but as is sometimes the case with Neopolitans, he bargained hard. He explained that the pony must be transported in an enormous van and the price of the transportation would be 25,000 lira ($300 at that time). She finally agreed to pay the price. On the day that the pony was to arrive, everyone awaited anxiously. A large Mercedes drove into the driveway. Two men were in front, two men in back, the cart on the top and the pony standing in the back of the Mercedes with his head sticking out of the window.

Wanda and I have become close friends. We are the same age, within a month, and we see each other as often as possible, on my trips to Italy and on hers to New York. I love her like a sister.

One Saturday we were driving from one of her country houses in Italy. It was a rainy day, and we had done a great deal of walking at an antique fair; so we dozed off in the car. She and I rode in the back seat and her chauffeur and Beatricia, the secretary of her houses, sat in the front seat. As we drew near Florence, both Wanda and I woke from our car nap. She charmingly said, "Kay, we will always be friends now that we have slept together."

Jan Miner is one of the special people. She is extremely talented, amusing, kind, thoughtful, and she gets along with everyone. She is a rare phenomenon: An actress without an overactive ego, and she always has work.

Years ago Monsanta asked me to speak at a sales meeting for them. I agreed to write a script if *Vogue* would hire a good actress to do the actual recording. If I did it for one company, I would be expected to do it for others. Jan Miner was selected, and even though it was at a much lesser rate than her accustomed fee, she agreed to take the job.

I had admired Jan's work on T.V. from the time she had been a regular on the old "Robert Montgomery Presents."

She had been doing these voice jobs for *Vogue* for some time and yet we had not met. One day I was walking my dog on Beekman Place, when I came face to face with Jan and her pug dog, "Mister." I introduced myself, and both of us laughed. We had not met; yet, she

116

and Dick Merrill, her husband lived at 10 Mitchell Place, just around the corner from me. We talked and started visiting and she, Dick, and I have been friends ever since. They introduced me to Sylvia Sidney - who was a neighbor of mine in Roxbury - Eileen Heckert, and Myrna Loy. We celebrate every occasion we can think of, and Jan sent me opening night tickets to all her plays. I even invested in *The Women*, a play that was greatly helped by Jan's role as the Countess DeLage. She played it as a wall-to-wall drunk, a role Jan says she understands quite well.

One birthday the Slavins had a party for me at their Roxbury home. Jan and Dick arrived tired and a little late from New York. They had a home in Bethel, Connecticut, at that time. Jan informed Maeve that she was on a diet and could drink only water. At some point during the evening, no one knows exactly when, she grew weary of water and switched to vodka. They looked the same, so we were surprised when Jan disappeared. She had gone to the bathroom and wasn't able to get up. It took both Dick and Sylvia Sidney to get her to the car. Jan is seldom, if ever, mean when drunk. Instead she is exceedingly amusing. She sometimes becomes another person, a countess with a Russian accent. Dick can ask her the most difficult questions, and she always gives a learned reply...things she doesn't seem to know when sober. We've decided that she must have this countess buried somewhere in her psyche, or was one in a former life.

Those who know Jan love her, and a great many love her who don't even know her, judging from her mail, and the people waiting for her at the stage door. She makes me feel good when I see her, or even when we talk on the phone.

Jan tells me marvelous tales. She is witty and not afraid to tell a story on herself.

Another year, again on my birthday, which always seems to fall on the coldest, bleakest day in January, Jan and Dick had a dinner party for me and then took the party to the opera to see Beverly Sills in *La Traviata* with Sara Caldwell conducting. I was enchanted by Caldwell. She totally ignored her more than ample shape, and handled herself with grace. She has a devotion to her work that is delightful to watch. Sills was a smash, but sweet Sara stole the show.

117

Jan and Dick have wonderful parties. The food and wine are superb, and the guest list beautifully balanced. Their country home in Bethel, Connecticut, was like a movie set. It was filled with antique treasures, and built around a charming pool. Dick who is an actor, a writer, and a producer, a set designer for the movies and T.V. (*Rachel, Rachel, Marigolds and Gamma Rays, Johnny, We Hardly Knew Thee*) did the restoration of their old house and made several additions. Every corner was an interesting setting.

They have a large circle of friends and it is not unusual for someone to meet an ex-husband or wife at the Merrills. It hasn't happened to me yet, but who knows.

In addition to playing the drunken countess in *The Women*, Jan was in *Saturday, Sunday and Monday*, and *The Heiress* with Richard Kiley and Jane Alexander. She has played the role of Madge on T.V. for Palmolive for twenty-two years. She is equally at home doing Shakespeare, Shaw, and T.S. Eliot. In the movie, *Lenny*, she played Lenny Bruce's mother.

At the American Shakespeare company at Stratford, Connecticut, Jan has played many demanding roles: as Mistress Quickly in *The Merry Wives of Windsor*, as Emilia in *Othello*, the Widow of Florence in *All's Well That Ends Well*, as well as Lady Britomart in Shaw's *Major Barbara*.

In addition to Jan's easy delightful wit, she gives freely of her time and praise to others. When speaking of Martin De Costa who signed her to *The Women*, she says, "He was enormous help to me, one of the finest directors with whom I have worked. I'm certain that Myrna Loy was responsible for my being hired in the first place. I know she impressed the producers."

The first time that Myrna Loy came to my old mill was a cold snowy winter's day. Shamus was a puppy, and he showed a puppy's enthusiasm when greeting guests by jumping on them. So that he wouldn't get his wet feet on Myrna I let him have his run while I dressed. It was my intention to have him inside when she and Jan arrived. While I was dressing, I looked out the window and saw Shamus jump the stone wall, cross the road and head for the woods. Neither of my other dogs had felt the need to leave their yard, so I was surprised and annoyed. Quickly I put on a storm coat and yellow rubber boots over my long Marimekko dress and ran toward my wandering dog. After trampling through the crusty snow for some time, Shamus and I finally arrived at the same spot at the same time. I brought him home but not before Jan drove in with Myrna. I looked a mess but Myrna was so charming, she put me at ease.

On Friday the 13th, I had a party and Jan, Dick, and Myrna were among the guests. I greeted them at the foot of the outside steps and thanked them for coming on this date. Myrna smiled and said, "It was Friday the 13th in 1925 that I signed my first contract with Warner Brothers." Only someone young and attractive would dare to admit it. This endeared Myrna to me and I have loved her since that day.

The Merrills had a party in their Bethel home preceding an evening with Lillian Gish at the Stratford Shakespearean Theater. Generous drinks were enjoyed and then the group drove to the theater. Maeve had gone with me and we were not too thrilled at Miss Gish's bad quality old movies. Also we had a long drive back to Roxbury, so we decided the next time the lights were dimmed we would flee.

The following day, on her way shopping, Maeve stopped by my mill. I was having a swim in the pool when the phone rang. Maeve asked should she answer it and I said yes. The voice on the other end said, "Kay, this is Lillian Gish. I noticed that you left early last night. I wanted you to know that I will be lecturing next week in Stanford. You can come and hear the finish." Maeve thanked Miss Gish and called me to come speak with her. When I took the phone, Jan was enjoying a good laugh. She had impersonated Miss Gish's voice so well that she had us both fooled.

One of the things the Merrills and I have in common besides dogs is food, and trying to diet. Jan says we should start a "Prayer for Proper Metabolism Group" for over 20's who are over 20.

Jan tells a story about herself and her diets. She was called to New England to fill in for an actress, in a starring role, who had become ill. It was a well-known fact that the star was somewhat thinner than Jan, but those in charge believed that Jan could do almost anything, including a crash weekend diet.

She was put on a small dinner, given a few lettuce leaves now and then while she learned her lines. The theater was dark on Monday so she had three days to learn the entire script and to aim toward fitting into the wardrobe. All was going well including the diet when a wonderful smell came from the kitchen. Jan rushed to the cook, inquired what produced this glorious aroma and he told her it was a pecan pie. Without a moment's hesitation she said, "I'll take it." With that she sat and ate the whole thing.

> *Jan and Dick's Dessert*
> *Here's one of our "once a year desserts" for a thin season.*
> *10 Macaroons*
> *3 T. Grand Marnier*
> *2 T. Orange Juice*
> *5 eggs*
> *2/3 C sugar*
> *3 more T. Grand Marnier (and still more to come)*
> *1 grated orange rind (fine)*
> *2 C. heavy cream*
> *3/4 C. Grand Marnier*
> *In a bowl, mix 10 macaroons, 3 T. Grand Marnier and 2 T. orange juice and mash.*
> *Separate the 5 eggs. Keep 4 whites. Beat egg yolks with 2/3 C. sugar until thick and light. Stir in 3 T. Grand Marnier and grated rind of one orange. Fold in 2 C. whipped cream and 4 egg whites beaten.*
> *Spread 1/2 of the macaroon paste on bottom of spring pan, pour 1/2 mixture into spring pan. Take remainder of paste layer on top. Pour in rest of mixture. Put in freezer 4 hours or more. Drink remainder of Grand Marnier.*
> *Thirty minutes before serving, release from spring pan and put on serving dish. When ready serve flambe.*

Mercedes Matter is a well-known artist, and Founder and past Director of the New York Studio School at 8 West 8th Street.

This school is a working environment for the study of art. A student who attends the New York Studio School must be totally involved with art. He should have more than the intention or the desire to be involved. He should have additionally, an already developed capacity, with some maturity in his working habits. I am well acquainted with this school because I served on the Board of Directors for several years.

Mercedes is a rare woman with deep perception, and a complete dedication to art and to the school she helped get started. Some have called her one of the most influential women in the American art world today. To me, she is a tender, talented, tormented humanitarian. She is a fabulous cook, a true and satisfying friend. She seldom arrives anywhere on time, sometimes even days late. A friend was invited to the Bethlehem, Connecticut, home of Mercedes and Herbert - her husband was a famous photographer and graphic artist - for Sunday dinner at seven. When the friend and her husband drove up the road to the Matter home, they passed Mercedes' car headed in the opposite direction. She was leaving on a shopping trip for the evening meal. She corrected me by saying that she was going for the wine. Her meals are well worth the wait. Just watching Mercedes cook in her roomy old early American house, with two kitchens, is a glorious experience.

Since she was a small girl, Mercedes has been intimately involved with art and its growth in this country. She was a member of the club that helped bring in the great period of "Abstract Expressionism."

She is the daughter of a painter, Arthur B. Carles. Mercedes speaks of him with feeling and intensity:

> "By 1926 he was painting abstractions prophetic of the late forties and early fifties. My father was fascinating, an extremely erratic father. At times he was infinitely sensitive and tender... When I visited him in Philadelphia as a young child he would put me in his studio, with canvas and palette set up, and leave me alone for several hours. Returning, he would delight in what I had

121

painted, once taking my painting directly to an exhibition where he was showing. It was bought by the cellist Hans Kindler...Earl Horter, one of my father's close friends, had the first collection of cubism in America. I remember sitting for hours while they talked surrounded by those brown paintings which did not appeal to me. One, a Picasso, now at the Museum of Modern Art, became the one compensation. It was red, green, black and white."

After attending Bennett College, Mercedes studied art with Hans Hofmann at the Art Students League.

"Studying with Hofmann opened the world of art for me. There is a threshold to cross which is the crucial one — where one first identifies experience with the language of one's art. This happened to me through Hofmann — an enormous revelation which changed everything."

She once took Hofmann to Philadelphia to visit her father, whom he knew. Hofman and Carles spoke together for thirty-six hours, without a break for sleep. Each man was starved for talk, with a peer, about art.

During the time of the W.P.A. Mercedes got a job on the Art Project. She was one of the small group on the project that was chosen to work with Fernand Leger. Others were McNeil and de Kooning. Mercedes was the only woman on the Leger project and also the only one who spoke French. She said that her translations for Leger lead to a friendship and she invited him to Philadelphia to visit her father. When they passed mountains of wrecked cars in North Philadelphia, Leger got up and jumped up and down in the aisle of the train because he was so transported by the spectacle.

It was during this period that the American Abstract Artists was started. This group, the majority of whose members had been students of Hofmann, was formed to exhibit together.

Leger brought Herbert Matter, a Swiss photographer, and Mercedes together. Herbert was in charge of display at the Swiss Pavilion at the World Fair in 1939. He hired Mercedes and it was not long after that they fell in love and married in the spring of 1941.

During the war years many European artists were living in New York and the city was very much alive. Jose Luis Sert organized a weekly evening at the Jumble Shop on 8th Street. Many of the artists met there: Leger, Hayther, the Calders and others. The Calders were then special friends of Herbert and continued to be so until Sandy's death.

In 1942 Leger came to New York, lived with the Matters and painted in Herbert's studio. A year later the Matters and their small son, Alex, moved to California so that Herbert could work with Charles Eames. They left the studio with Leger but with the war rationing of coal, he found it too cold and moved out. This left the Matters without a studio when they returned from California three years later.

Mercedes felt exiled in California. She missed being in the world of artists. In the late forties de Kooning had his first show, and it had a crucial impact on them.

> "Each evening, around midnight, I would do
> my shopping at the vegetable and fruit stand at 6th
> Avenue and 8th Street, and on the way home stop
> in at the 'Waldorf,' a cafeteria where the painters
> used to go for coffee and a bite after painting.
> Around that time Mothersell's Studio 35 was
> formed, a school and a catalyst for the emergence
> of the New York School because there, for the first
> time, a forum was created in which artists spoke to
> the artists community...de Kooning, Cage, Barney
> Newman. Somehow this brought people and
> ideas together, created a climate which issued in
> the great period of abstract expressionism."

123

Not long afterward the Artist's Club was formed to replace the Waldorf Cafeteria as a meeting place. Mercedes said "The Club" was marvelous.

> "It brought together in one place, at on time, the greatest diversity of artists: Edwin Dickinson, Earl Kerkam, Franz Kline, William de Kooning, Philip Guston, Brodley Walker Tomlin, Barney Newman, Harold Rosenberg, John Cage, Morton Feldman, Dylan Thomas, Edgar Verose and many others. I was the only original female member, having been one of the habitue' of the Waldorf. There was extraordinary warmth and camaraderie among artists there. The end of the marvelous time came when American art became big business. Success seemed to spoil the climate. During the good time, and for some years thereafter, the Cedar Bar was also a meeting place. For two years I spent my nights there, I listened and learned a great deal. Kline was always there. For a time Guston and Tomlin were my constant companions. This was one of the most exciting periods of my life."

The summers were spent in Easthampton or the Hamptons, which gradually became the summer art world. Mercedes and Herbert went because the Pollocks, whom they had known before, lived there. Gradually the artists came. Leo Castelli took a house, and de Kooning painted there one summer. Herbert made a film on Calder during one of the summers, using the sea with many of Calder's works.

This was a time when there were miles of unspoiled beach, where one could go and see no one.

Mercedes began teaching art first at the Philadelphia College of Art and then Pratt Institute. She was shocked to find that the students painted primarily in class only.

"When I studied, we had worked everyday with periodic instruction. This new way was a farce. And of course, it became soon apparent that the serious and talented students were utterly miserable and frustrated. This began to prey on my mind. I decided to write an article exposing the absurdity of the situation so that I would not have to think of it anymore."

"What's Wrong with U.S. Art Schools," was published in *Art News*, September, 1963. It was a bombshell.

Students came to Mercedes one night with the idea of creating a real art school and asked for her help. The founding students were from her classes at Pratt and Philadelphia. The idea of creating a school occurred around January 1964.

There were problems. They needed a faculty, money, a building. The school opened September 21, 1964, with sixty students from various parts of the country in a loft.

Mercedes went to her friends, the artists she most admired, and persuaded them to serve as her faculty. She also asked Meyer Shapiro, and explained that he was the one art historian who had found communion with the artists. He agreed to help, and he continues to be a crucially important element in the school.

The Kaplan Fund was the first to give support to the school but only on the condition that there be a Board of Trustees.

Herbert occupied Gertrude Whitney's studio on MacDougal Alley at this time. In 1966, he told Mercedes that the entire complex of buildings which had comprised the original Whitney Museum, including his studio, was to go on the market.

During the fall of 1966 a student of the school died suddenly. When she reached her twenty-first birthday she had made a will leaving half her estate to the school. This money made it possible to buy the old Whitney Museum at 8 West 8th Street where the school is still alive and doing well.

On October 7, 1986, there was a reception at the New York Studio School for an exhibition of the Founding Faculty. There were fourteen well known artists in this show: Cajori, Carone, Dickinson, Geist, Guston, Heliker, Katz, Kerkam, Finkelstein, Matter, Murch, Schapiro, Spanenta, Vincente.

Mercedes is an unusual cook. She makes the simplest dishes taste better than they have any right to taste. Many is the time that I have enjoyed a superb beef stew that I always associate with her. She told me that she got the recipe originally from Louisa Calder, the wife of Alexander Calder, but she has doubtless added touches of her own.

> *Mercedes Matters' Beef Stew*
> *2 lbs. beef cut for stew*
> *2 jars of pimentos*
> *1/4 lb. black olives*
> *4 carrots cut up or 10 small carrots*
> *8 small white onions*
> *garlic — much, in my case*
> *olive oil*
> *salt and pepper to taste*
> *red wine*
> *Brown sliced garlic in oil in frying pan. Brown beef chunks in oil and garlic. Put browned beef chunks in stew pot (I use an enameled iron pot.) Add vegetables and cover amply with red wine. Simmer until meat is tender. (Better the following day.)*

In my opinion, and just about the opinion of everyone else, Geoffrey Beene is the man of the hour in the fashion world. He is gentle, brilliant, sensitive, and is overflowing with talent. In addition he is a workaholic.

The first time we got well acquainted was at a luncheon arranged by Elsa Klensch, at that time a fashion editor at *Vogue*. Geoffrey wanted to design a line of shoes under his name, so Elsa got us together. We had immediate rapport. He talked about his life in

Louisiana and how he started out to be a doctor and then turned to design. I adored him and have ever since that day. We have become good friends and I treasure the friendship.

He told me that he had a passion for shoes as long as he could remember and was anxious to get involved with the designs of women's shoes. When he was a small boy he went without lunch for several weeks without telling his mother in order to buy a pair of clogs for himself. He said that he just had to have them. Shoes were always a passion for him.

Bert Geller of Andrew Geller had for many years been a favorite of mine. He was attractive and intelligent. I liked him, his approach to business, to fashion and to me. A few months before there had been a meeting between Calvin Klein and Bert for the same purpose. The Calvin Klein clothes are cheaper than Beene's, so naturally the shoes would be cheaper. Today U.S. Shoe Corporation makes the Calvin Klein shoes. I felt that the association of Geller and Beene would be good for both of them and not conflict with Calvin's shoes. I phoned Bert and he, Geoffrey, and I had breakfast together that week. They got along well and after melon and tea, I left them together to work out the details. Each one talked with me separately about the affiliation. Contracts were finally signed and the marriage with Andrew Geller lasted seventeen years. There was a line under the Beene name and a less expensive line under the Beenebag name.

In addition to Geoffrey's large gift for good design, he makes clothes with the woman in mind. They can be worn by a small person, a thin or ample woman, and they fit well into a life-style. His clothes are made to be worn rather than just admired and hung in a closet.

On October 15, 1976, he became the first American designer to show and manufacture his clothes in Europe. He showed his new line in Milan, Italy. The same styles that were made in America were manufactured in Italy for the European market. His designs have an American flavor, but he mostly uses Italian fabrics, so the marriage was well-suited. I would like to share an explanation about Geoffrey in Italy. The quote below came with my invitation to attend the opening.

"When one speaks of Beene they speak of style. This exists in all his creative endeavors. What does Beene design other than ready-made clothing for women: Furs, scarves, handbags, shoes, jewels, luggage, glasses, stockings, and, of course, all his accessories for sportswear. His name, and commitment, have been given enthusiastically to men's fashion, both in tennis and clothing as well. He launched a new cologne for men in America, and called it "Grey Flannel." He was awarded, by the Fragrance Foundation of America, in June of this year, the award for best introduction of a new man's fragrance and packaging."

I appreciate Geoffrey's talent and admire him tremendously but I'm not sure I know what makes him run. Last week I asked him and he said, "I don't know myself." I rather feel he does.

This spring Wanda Ferragamo, and her daughter Giovanna came to Roxbury for the weekend. Saturday evening I had a small dinner party: Alexander and Tatiana Liberman, Molly and Joe Reed, Wanda and Giovanna, Virginia Coigney, and Geoffrey Beene. Maeve Slavin and Patrick, her 14 year old son came for drinks. It was catered by Bill and Doug of "Today's." The menu included a smoked salmon I had brought from the city from Barney Greengrass, "The Sturgeon King," and fresh asparagus for the hors d'oeuvre. The asparagus were peeled, served on a silver tray with a sour cream dip.

Then a clear fish soup with lobster and crabmeat.

The main course was slices of pink tenderloin circled on a large platter by spinach crepes that were twice folded. Bill passed carrots and other vegetables. The salad was topped by fiddle ferns (available only at this season).

Both red and white wine was served with the meal.

The dessert was pink grapefruit cold souffle with sugar cookies. With the dessert I served champagne.

After dinner we had freshly ground coffee, and brandy in the living room before the fire.

It rained the day of the party. Geoffrey had stopped by at the Liberman's, in Warren, to see their lovely house and the sculpture yard where Alex works. The yard is a feast for the eyes. It is filled with enormous designs made of steel. The Ferragamos and I went the next day and, even though I have seen it several times, it constantly changes. I found it difficult to leave the excitement of his sculpture.

Geoffrey came from the rain into my mill by the side door that opens into the dining room. His chauffeur, Frank, followed carrying a large white quince tree too tall even to stand in my low ceilinged mill. Geoffrey quietly said, "I don't think it will do for the table." The tree was planted in the yard in a spot chosen by Wanda and it has flourished. Sometime later when Frank was driving me home from the Beene showroom, I asked him how that tree fit into Geoffrey's Rolls Royce. He said it had been necessary to remove one of the front seats in order to do so.

Flowers are an important part of Geoffrey's life. He has large orchid filled greenhouses on his Oyster Bay estate and he spends his happiest moments working with his flowers.

Almost every week when both of us are in town, Geoffrey and I have dinner together. We both enjoy good food, eating early, and finding good restaurants. Mimi Sheratorn is a friend of each of us and she tells us about interesting restaurants. Mimi wrote a book with Alan King that had a great deal of humor in it. When the book didn't do as well as anticipated, Mimi came to the conclusion that people are serious about food and do not want to think about it in a laughing, frivolous way.

Geoffrey has a special relationship to unusual and beautiful fabrics. Not only are his designs original, young and appealing, but his taste is on a high level. He has the capacity of combining little touches that delight him in countries where he visits such as Japan and Austria with the strong American flavor that runs through all his clothes. His work has a refinement that reflects his personality. They are easy to wear and they do not overpower a woman who wears them.

In Caroline Reynolds Milbank's book called *Couture*, she spoke of Beene:

> "He showed his creativity with fabrics early on, choosing ones that had previously been thought of as formal and combining them with those that had previously been used only for day, resulting in a relaxed elegance. In 1967, for example, he showed dresses printed in a houndstooth plaid, inset with undulating bands of lace — a fresh approach that still surfaces in his collections and has done more to invigorate the reputation of lace."

I asked Geoffrey, who is knowledgeable about foods and restaurants, to share his five favorite restaurants with us. They are:

Cent Anni — Carmine Street, New York City
Mr. Chow's — London
King Tsien — Honolulu
Arnaud's — New Orleans
Le Cafetiere — Paris

Geoffrey also gave me some thoughts on food:

> "My first memories of food came from my family garden — that even preceded my awareness of flowers. But somehow breads are the most memorable of tastes — cornbread, spoonbread, hoecakes, buttermilk biscuits, yeast rolls — were all unforgettable. Breads are my undoing — not sweets. When I do diet it is bread that I miss the most. I do believe that breads are one of the simplest foods that I enjoy that has been tampered with the least with today's cooks. Until I left my small town for the University of New Orleans most of my tastebuds had experienced the robustness and simplicity of Provincial food. That initial experience remains my first choice of both restaurants and cuisine. Once in New Orleans I was to

learn the absolute joy of one of the great cuisines of America — the Creole. It has never traveled or translated well to other parts of America or Europe. Its flavor when perfected is as unique, subtle and pure as any fine cuisine in all the world. I make one annual trip to New Orleans to ravish the ultimate sophistication of its delicacies, then to France to witness the height of indulgence in food. Due to my background I still prefer the humble bistro to the grand restaurant. There is less code and more taste. Back to New York and the seemingly endless culinary conventions in the New York "potpourri." I agree with Mimi Sheratorn that to eat well and in good company is one of the great pleasures of life. I cannot cook but have a library of over 500 cookbooks for the references of all good friends and cooks who come to my country home to delight me."

Listed below are four of Geoffrey Beene's favorite recipes:

Mexican Cornbread
1 C. yellow cornmeal
1/2 T. salt
1/2 T. soda
1/3 C. melted shortening
1 (8 oz.) carton sour cream
1 can (8 oz.) creamed corn
2 eggs beaten
1 C. shredded cheddar cheese
1 (4 oz.) can chopped green chiles
Combine cornmeal, salt, soda. Blend well. Stir in shortening.
Add sour cream, corn and eggs, mix well.
Spoon half of batter into greased heated 8 or 9 inch heavy skillet.
Sprinkle with cheese and chilies.

Cover with remaining mixture.

Bake at 375 degrees for 35 - 40 Minutes until golden brown.

Smothered Chicken
1 fryer (2 1/2 lbs.)
1/2 C flour
1/2 T. salt
dash of pepper
fat for frying
1 3/4 C. milk

Brown as for fried chicken. Pour off all but about 2 T. of fat. Stir in 1/8 C. remaining seasoned flour. Add milk, heat to boiling, stirring constantly. Return chicken to pan, cover and simmer 1 1/2 hours or until tender.

Shrimp Macaroni Salad
3 cans of small shrimp (4 or 5 oz. each)
2 C. of cooked shell macaroni
1 C. chopped raw cauliflower
1 C. of sliced celery
1/4 C. of chopped sweet pickles, or drained pickle relish
1/2 C. mayonnaise or salad dressing
3 T. garlic french dressing
1 T. lemon juice
1 tsp. grated onion
1 tsp. celery seed
1 tsp. salt
1/4 tsp. pepper
salad greens
1 hard boiled egg, sliced

Drain shrimp, let stand in ice water for about 5 minutes. Drain (cut shrimp in half if large). Combine macaroni, cauliflower, celery, parsley, pickles, and shrimp. Combine

132

mayonnaise, French dressing, lemon juice, onion and sea-
soning, mix well. Add mayonnaise mixture to shrimp and toss
lightly. Chill. Serve on salad greens, garnish with egg slices.
Serves 6.

Dirty Rice
1/2 C. chopped onion
1/2 C. celery
1/2 C. green peppers
1 can mushroom soup
1 can beef consomme
1 C. water
1 C. rice
1/2 tsp. salt
1 stick of oleo margarine

Saute onions, celery, peppers, in oleo. Mix all ingredients
and put in covered casserole. Bake 1 hour at 375 degrees. Stir
occasionally.

Wanda Ferragamo

Geoffrey Beene

Armi Ratia

Mercedes Matter
Artist and Founder of New York Studio School of Art

Richard Merell

Jan Miner, Actress

Teddy and Arthur Edelman

Shamus watching TV

Ruth and Skitch Henderson

Faux Pas and Foibles

Almost everyone puts her foot in her mouth more times than she likes to remember. This is one exercise in which I excel. I'm accomplished, experienced, and a past master at stumbling over my own feet. Regardless of how often it has happened, it's seldom, if ever, easy to take.

At a *Vogue* party in my suite at the Ambassador East in Chicago, some years ago, I noticed a rather small man was talking on my phone for about thirty minutes. I needed the phone to be free so guests could call and inquire about the party. Also the little man was totally unknown to me. After ten more minutes of watching him monopolize my phone, I lost my patience and without thinking, turned to a slight man close by and demanded, "Who in the hell is that little man using my phone?" Without blinking an eyelash the slight man said, "He's my brother."

Anna Winteur, a special lady, came to *Vogue* from *New York Magazine*. She is bright and talented, but her experience with shoe pages was somewhat limited. My feeling is that unless pages featuring shoes have the human element of a face, a hand or a beautiful leg, they must be somewhat close up in a still life that is artistic and shows the details, textures, and silhouette. Shoe pages must be animated, brought to life or else they are just shoes, nothing more.

Each March I do my what I call block-buster group of spring shoe pages. Anna's first try at getting a special new photographer to do these pages was a sad and disappointing experience for me. The shoes did not excel, and I felt the pages were dry and stilted. Because she was new I didn't want to say anything to her, but I fretted and stewed for several sleepless nights wondering how I could solve my problem. I knew I must use caution and tread lightly if we were to have a compatible working relationship. Robert Turner, a *Vogue* editor at that time had been on the sitting, and he walked into my office at a time when my patience had expired. He asked me how I liked my pages and without thinking I firmly replied, "I hate them, I hate them." He was crushed and immediately went to Anna and told her I hated my pages.

Anna asked me if I had said I hated my pages. I would have preferred to have discussed the matter with her in a less forceful way, but had to admit what I had said.

She asked me to sit and air my feelings. I insisted that she wouldn't like them, but she assured me that she liked strong women and welcomed my views. We had a lengthy conversation about my expectations for my pages and what years of experience had taught me concerning the emotion, the drama, the energy I expect in my pages. They should all be different but have a part of me in each of them. I like pages with tempo, feeling, beauty, and energy. They need to be of value to a larger segment of designers, manufacturers, retailers than those shown in actual pages, they should be trend setting, and they should have action.

Anna was magnificent. She listened, did not seem offended and at that moment we became fast friends. She later became Editor-in-Chief of English *Vogue*, and I had dinner at Claridge's in London in September with Anna and her husband.

A number of friends of mine have word processors for writing; not me. I'm not fond of mechanical equipment, and my mind can't keep its train of thought while I struggle to type them. Actually I type fairly well, but I've dictated my work for so many years the typing has become rusty. Kady was offered money to take dictation for the book, but felt she did not have the time; so I write with a pen on a large lined pad.

When I was searching in a cabinet for writing pads I found an article Maeve Slavin had written in the New Milford *Times* about Shamus watching T.V. Not only was he addicted to T.V. but he even knew the theme music of commercials that had animals in them. Several times we were in the yard or on the first floor when he rushed upstairs and seated himself before the tube, waiting to see the Chuck Wagon or cats on Kitty Vittles. I couldn't believe that he knew the music; so I followed him several times, only to find that he did and that he sat glued before the screen until the animals appeared.

In the same article, which was accompanied by a delightful picture of Shamus, Maeve told of walking him to the paper store in New York, where she encountered a large bulldog that was one of his number one enemies. He reared up on his hind legs and barked wildly. While she was trying to decide what might subdue this wild monster, Jan Miner came out of the paper store and exclaimed, "Why Shamus, I thought I recognized your voice." He immediately recognized hers and ran happily to her side, hoping that she had not seen him acting badly.

Shamus had not seen a horse close up except on T.V.; however, he barked at every one from the country to the city, and since we drove through Westchester horse country, he was extremely vocal. There were times when this became annoying, but I did not seem able to control his barking even when he saw horses at great distances. One day I took him to a vet in Southbury, and there was a horse out back. I asked the owner if she objected to my dog getting close to her horse. When Shamus got near the horse he looked awestruck and was completely quiet. From that day forward he never barked at horses again. I reasoned that he had not imagined a horse would be so large, and that he felt over matched. He gave up one passion for a more modern one — motorbikes.

When I think of Karen Hubert I think of *Alice in Wonderland*. I'm not quite sure why. Both of them had long hair, both are wide-eyed, interested in just about everything. Karen has since cut her hair, but she is still fey, appealing and delightful. She looks and carries herself like a dancer.

Leo Lerman, who was the Features Editor of *Vogue* at the time, went to dinner at a charming restaurant at 102 East 22nd called Hubert's. He liked the food, the quality, the ambience, so he wrote a small flattering review of his visit in *Vogue*. Soon people from all parts, including me, were going there. I liked it immediately. Also I thought Karen and Len Allison, who ran the kitchen, were special. They are now married.

Karen has become a special friend, also a well-known star in the food world. She and Len were living in Brooklyn Heights. Both were working and each of them had always been interested in food. They needed $5,000 for a new camera necessary for their work, so they decided to serve special meals in their living room on the weekend. Almost from the beginning, word spread and they were filled with customers. This was roughly twelve years ago. They continued this in-house restaurant for a year and enjoyed it so much they gave up their jobs in television and education and opened a restaurant in a bar. During the year they were there, Mimi Sheraton reviewed them in the New York *Times*. From then on, everything grew like topsy. Soon after, they bought their present location off Park Avenue on 22nd Street.

I asked Karen to talk about the beginning of their restaurant and to include several recipes:

"I loved to eat and cook. Not only was cooking a challenge, it represented a world of style and elegance. Cooking was a door into a wider sphere of sophistication. As much as I loved food I found even more exciting its power to evoke The Good Life: The world of *Vogue*, Bentleys, summers on the Riviera and all the fine things in life that were too rich for me but so deliciously worth having. If I couldn't own them, at least I could taste them.

"I never expected to become a professional cook. I enjoyed dinner company. Temperamentally I liked pleasing people and the idea of service was not foreign to me. In my fantasies I thought I might be happy owning a restaurant.

"I would be able to eat the best food whenever I wanted. There would be lots of shadowy people, like waiters and managers, to do the other things like taking coats, crumbing tables, making sure the bills were paid, and making money. This last little detail, making money, was something I had little interest in until the autumn of 1976.

"Len and I had careers. He worked in television film and I worked in education. We were working on a project together and needed an expensive camera. We began to think of ways to earn the money for that camera. What we needed, we decided, was our own small business. But first we needed to decide on the product we wanted to sell.

"That fall we were walking along the Promenade in Brooklyn Heights and noticed that the food vendors were doing quite well. Coffee, pretzels, hot dogs, shishkebabs, falafels were selling out in the chilly autumn air. Then, given Brooklyn's overdeveloped interest in things domestic and culinary (it is, after all, the borough of brownstones and one-family homes), we began to notice middle-class vendors with signs that read, 'Hot cocoa made with milk and droste chocolate — $1.75,' and 'Jarlesberg and Black Forest ham sandwiches on fresh baked pumpernickel — $3.25.' There was even 'Best chocolate chip cookies in Brooklyn, home baked by Prospect Heights mom — $1.50.'

"The next Sunday morning we set out for the Promenade Art Show with leftovers from our Saturday night dinner. These were not just any old leftovers. We had some dinner guests the night before and I had prepared my favorite Simone Beck recipes: Pork au Bourbon, potato lychettes and Gateau chocolate with scotch and raisins. With some prodding from Len I had prepared an extra cake, several extra pounds of pork and potato lychettes. We sliced these fancy 'leftovers,' arranged them carefully on pretty antique platters and wrote our sign, 'Gourmet French Food, Porc au Bourbon, 75 cents a slice. Rich Chocolate Cake — $1.00.' In a few hours we had sold all our food.

"In the afternoon, some very nice ladies asked us if we ever did dinner parties. First we were complimented. Then we were delighted with the idea. We went home, encouraged. If people thought we were good enough to cook for their dinner parties, perhaps we could hire ourselves out.

"Len and I never meant to start a restaurant, but we ended up with one! Before the fall of 1976 neither of us had ever considered entering the restaurant business. Restaurants were special treats that belonged to the world of celebrities and rewards.

"Where were we when we were not dining out? Dining in of course. Cooking at home was a relaxing therapy, an escape from the pressures of work, a creative activity that was its own reward. Like many other cooking-romantics, food held a spell over us that was pure magic.

"I cooked simple French dishes. Scallops of veal in cream and calvados, braised endive, sweet and fruity pork dishes like Simone Beck's Porc au Bourbon with pitted prunes. I loved sweet desserts, chocolate tortes, and frozen mousse. I had no collection of fancy gadgets. I owned no blender, no double boiler, no cuisinart. A garlic press and an egg beater were all my kitchen could boast. For all the cooking I did I had not yet mastered the art of sharpening knives: I was still cutting with serrated edges. No graduate of carbon steel or Solingen was I. I had one copper bottomed skillet, an old Wearever whose handle had worn off, that my mother had given me years before.

"It was Len who saw further possibilities. Instead of going to someone else's home, why not have dinner parties in our house instead?

"We still had bills to pay, and we needed a new camera. Perhaps this was our business-on-the-side. We could turn our house into a small private dining club on the weekends. We could start by inviting friends and we could cook the dishes I knew best, things that were sure to be successful and enjoyable. We'd make a sumptuous feast, a five course meal. We owned very little furniture, but we did have three tables: Our round oak dining table, a butcher block on saw legs that we used for editing tape and a small antique drafting table big enough for two people. We owned eight chairs and perhaps my parents would lend us some dishes and flatware.

"We began by looking through our address book. We gathered the names of fifty friends and acquaintances. Some of these were close or old friends, but most were people we knew from teaching and television.

"We handwrote fifty invitations. We described time, place, food and promised a five course meal for $8.50 — no gratuity, please. We reasoned that diners were guests in our home, even though they were paying. We kept this no tip policy for the following ten months we ran the restaurant in our home.

"That first weekend twenty-two people came to eat dinner — eleven on Saturday and eleven on Sunday. Since it had sold out on the Promenade and had always been successful at dinner parties, we again turned to Simone Beck's Porc au Bourbon.

"The meal was hearty and delicious. Both evenings were successful. Everyone had a good time and when we deducted our food costs we discovered that we had made a profit. Best of all, we hadn't had to stand out in the cold. The money we had made was our own, tax free and pure profit. We had no overhead.

"We decided to do it again. That Monday and Tuesday we called up each of the twenty-two people who had come to dinner and asked everyone of them for the names and addresses of four or five friends of theirs who might enjoy the experience of a home cooked dinner.

"By developing a mailing list in this way, we were able to continue our business in our home for nearly a year. Most of the people who came enjoyed their experience enough to give us the names and addresses of some of their friends. Sometimes customers would call us unsolicited and volunteer the names of friends. New people came all the time. For most, the evening eating in our home was a lark. As our operation became more successful and sophisticated, diners' expectations grew. They came to our home to eat food that was a little better or more complex than what they cooked for themselves at home.

"The price was right. For $8.50 to $10.50, people could bring their own wines, ask for seconds, and stay all night. The people who came to our home tended to be adventurous eaters. Our little operation proved Mr. Vallato's favorite theory: As long as the food is good, people will go anywhere for a meal.

"Most of our customers came from Manhattan. Our food was good enough and our home was quaint enough so that even the most dour pilgrim who had been dragged over across The Great Bridge by a curious wife or friend was satisfied.

"Our home was inviting and warm. We lived in a three-story Mews House that had six small rooms, two to each floor. We did not own much furniture, so that most of the rooms we had turned into dining areas had plenty of space for tables and

141

chairs. Our walls were pleasantly decorated with antique quilts, authentic old farm tools, a few good nineteenth century paintings and one wall was covered by an exotic shell collection.

"The tables were set with antique china, stemware and family silver donated by my Aunt Cleo. We used old lace and linen tablecloths. The overall effect was of a picturesque if somewhat unconventional setting. There was a lot of love in that house and I think that visitors could feel it and were comfortable there."

Below are a number of Karen's recipes:

Country Captain Chicken
Curry Mixture
2 T. cumin
2 T. coriander seeds
4 bay leaves
1 cinnamon stick
1 T. black peppercorns
1 T. fennel seed
1 tsp. ground tumeric
1 T. mustard seed
1/2 tsp. all spice
1 tsp. black pepper
1 tsp. cayenne

Vegetables
2 tomatoes peeled, seeded & diced
1 red pepper - julienne
1 green pepper - julienne
3 scallion thin sliced
1 T. currents
1 medium onion

Grind all spices together and hold in a closed jar. Split and quarter a 3 lb. chicken. Trim off excess fat, remove wing tips and back. Reserve for making stock. Salt, pepper and lightly flour the chicken parts and brown until golden in saucepan with oil. Remove parts and pour oil, leaving enough to saute 1 medium onion diced, 1 tsp. garlic, 2 tsp. curry powder. Deglaze with 1/4 C. white wine. Add 3/4 C. chicken stock, 2 T. chutney and vegetables. Bring to a boil. Put chicken back in and cover and bake for 10 minutes. Remove from oven. Take out breast so that it doesn't overcook and reduce liquid over high flame. When thick add 1 T. batter, salt to taste and replace breast from which bone has been removed. Serve with basmati rice. Garnish sauce with toasted slivered almonds.

Roquefort Souffle
Heat 1 1/2 C. milk

Stir into a roux of 1 1/2 oz. butter, 1/3 C. flour, 1 T. cornstarch. Cool and whisk in 4 yolks and 1 C. blue cheese, crumbled and lightly packed. Add 2 T. cognac, 2 tsp. worcestershire and 5 drops tobasco sauce. Season with salt, pepper and nutmeg. Whip 4 whites or 1/2 C. of whites until soft peaks and fold into base. Ladle in cups that have been buttered and dusted with cornmeal. Bake in Bain marie for 20 minutes at 350 degrees. Serve with apple sauce and a little cream seasoned with salt, pepper and cognac and reduce slightly until thick.

Almond Brittle Ice Cream
Standard Ice Cream Base
2 C. milk scalded w/
1 split vanilla bean
Pour into
6 egg yolks ribboned with 3/4 C. sugar
pinch of salt

If the milk is hot enough and this operation is done quickly it is not necessary to cook the custard further although for smoother, richer consistency return the custard to the stove in a sauce pan and cook under a low heat while stirring continuously till thick or 160 degrees. Cool this custard.

Brittle
1 C. blanched almond slivers
1 1/2 C. sugar
Toast the almonds until golden on a sheet pan. Leave them spread evenly and pour over them the caramel made from the cup of sugar. Cool and break up with a knife. Add this to the ice cream base but reserve a few pieces for garnish. Whip 2 C. heavy cream to lightly mounting, but no peaks, and add to custard and brittle. Freeze. Serve with caramel sauce and brittle pieces.

Caramel Sauce
In a pan, brown 1 C. of sugar to caramel. Carefully add water to the hot sugar stirring continuously. At first the sugar will resist incorporating the water but gradually it will ease into a smooth sauce. Take it off the fire and add 1/4 C. cream and 1 T. butter. This gives it a glossy and opaque finish.

Karen took in a big beige dog who had been abused. She has worked wonders with him. I go to dinner at Hubert's as early as possible so I can have a brief visit with Ralph. He and I are friends; so I'm sure he won't mind me telling a story about one of his faux pas. Hubert's was catering a wedding reception for one of their backers. They had made a large tiered wedding cake and placed it in the wine room where it was cool and out of the way of the usual kitchen traffic. Ralph is allowed in Karen's office at times and usually seems content to sleep there. This day of the wedding someone had forgotten to close the wine room and Ralph entered, ate a section of each layer of the cake, then went back to his usual space, fat and filled. Up to this time Ralph's favorite food had been Hubert's home made bread.

When Karen was teaching him to walk on the lead, as well as trying to train him, she always carried a piece of bread to give him when he responded to her commands.

When the wine steward selected wine for the reception he noticed the disaster. It was too late to bake another cake. I asked Karen how she saved the day and she explained that she cut out any portion that had been near Ralph's mouth, filled in as best she could, redecorated and kept her mouth shut.

Jan Miner is well known as a non-cook. Her husband, Dick, is such a superb cook, so she leaves the cooking to him; however, one day she decided to cook prunes. She placed the prunes on the stove in a pan with water and went to her room to memorize a script. Sometime later she heard loud slashes on the door to her apartment, and rushed to make sure the door was not knocked down. When she opened it she found six firemen with axes raised and hoses ready to put out the fire. It seems that the prunes had burned sending smoke out her kitchen window. Someone had called the fire department and they were there ready to break down her front door and flood the apartment. Needless to say, Jan continues to leave the cooking to her husband Dick.

An Old Mill,
An Old Inn,
A New Puppy

I enjoy driving to a good restaurant in the winter or early autumn when the countryside is decorated by the colorful foliage. The best time to find the leaves at their peak in northwest Connecticut is usually the second week in October. Frost, the amount of rainfall, and the temperature have an effect on the exact timing.

Three years ago I allowed my old mill to be used by the Waterbury Y.W.C.A. for a house tour. The committee is composed of women from Waterbury and the villages near to it. I knew the chairman who had asked for the use of my house for several years so I finally consented. The committee took excellent care of each room. With the exception of heel prints and finger smears on the wall there was no damage to the house.

The date of the house tour was set for the second Sunday in October. I chose not to be present, so it was necessary to make other arrangements for Shamus and for me.

A friend and I, with Shamus, drove to Old Drovers Inn for lunch. Mr. Harris, the delightful manager of the restaurant, had repaired the fence that surrounded the back yard, so Shamus would not have to stay in the car. Everything seemed in order when we sat down for lunch, but I had not allowed for my deep feeling for the house. We had two drinks, and I began feeling worse rather than better. We drove home so I could lie down. When we got to within a half mile of the house, we saw the crowd. Hundreds of people were in line waiting for the tour. It was then I realized that at least part of my illness had come from thoughts of all those people walking through my mill. The house has a warm and cheerful atmosphere and I felt I had abused it by allowing all these people to go inside.

The crowds kept us from getting near the house, so we drove to Sylvia Sidney's house, close by.

Old Drovers Inn has been a favorite restaurant during the years that I have lived in Roxbury. It's not too far to drive, about forty-five minutes door to door, and well worth the trip.

It is one of the best restaurants anywhere, and by far the best in the vicinity of western Connecticut. Actually, it is in Dover Plains, New York, a village near the Connecticut border.

The Inn is an early American house built in 1750. It was used by the owners when sheep were driven through this section to market. The restaurant is on the lower ground level of the Inn. It has low black ceilings and a generous fireplace, facing the entrance. There is a large old bar to the left as you enter, and the tables circle around the fireplace. Food at Old Drovers is superb, beautifully prepared and served, and the menu offers a large choice; however, it tends to remain more or less the same. Prices are far from cheap but they do include tips. No credit cards are honored. At least one book on restaurants has listed Old Drovers Inn as one of the top ten restaurants in America. The menu is on a large hanging blackboard that is brought to each table.

The expresso at the Inn was delicious. I complimented Mr. Harris on its flavor. He said, "You know how we get it to taste that way, don't you? We make it with coffee instead of water."

Travis Harris III, the innkeeper came in 1945 as a bartender on weekends while he was attending Parson's School of Design. He graduated from Parson's in 1948 and went to live and work in Paris. In nine months he became disenchanted with Paris and the fashion world. Mr. Olin Potter, the owner of the Inn, offered Travis the job of manager of the Inn for the winter months.

Jim Potter, the present owner, gave me some tips and four recipes:

"Always make your expresso coffee with your regular dinner coffee taking the place of boiling water. Use the same amount of Medalia d'Oro as you normally would.

"To your regular mixture in deviled or stuffed eggs, add a bit of curry powder.

"Always use brown sugar in making Irish Coffee. In a twelve ounce stemmed wine goblet put one half tsp. brown sugar, add 3 oz. good Irish Whiskey and then fill with hot coffee to one inch below top of glass and then spoon on freshly made whipped cream that has a bit of brandy added to it rather than vanilla."

Old Drovers Inn Cheese Soup

4 T. butter

1/2 C. each, diced carrot, green pepper, minced onion, celery

1/3 C. flour

1 quart well-seasoned chicken stock (chicken bouillon cubes and water if no stock is available)

6 oz. young cheddar cheese, grated

6 oz. well-cured cheddar cheese, grated

3 to 4 C. very fresh milk

Salt and pepper

1) Melt butter in top of double boiler. Add vegetables and braise until tender, but not browned.

2) Blend in flour. Cook, stirring, one minute.

3) Add stock and cook, stirring till thickened.

4) Place over boiling water in lower part of double boiler, add cheese and cook, stirring, till cheese has melted.

5) Add enough milk to thin to consistency of cream. Season to taste with salt and pepper. Strain.

6) Reheat in double boiler. Serve hot, or in warm weather, chill and serve very cold. Yield about two quarts.

Old Drovers Inn Iced Lemon Soup a la Grecque

In a sauce pan combine 4 C. chicken stock and 2 C. light cream. Heat the mixture gently, stirring constantly, and stir in 2 T. cornstarch. Cook the soup over low heat without letting it boil until it begins to thicken. Beat 6 egg yolks lightly and briskly. Pour the egg yolk misture into the soup, add the juice of 8 lemons (1 C.), 1 tsp. monosodium glutamate, and a dash of cayenne. Let the soup cool and chill it for at least 8 hours. Serve the soup very cold, garnished with thin slices of lemon and chopped parsley. Makes 12 generous servings.

Old Drovers Inn iced Red Currant Soup
6 qts. fresh currants in cold water one inch above berries. Simmer for 30 minutes and then strain. Add two C. sugar, the juice of two lemons, 2 T. cinnamon, 1 C. dry red wine and one 8 oz. package of instant tapioca. Cook on a low fire for 30 minutes. Refrigerate for at least 6 hours and then serve in iced supreme bowl and garnish with 1 tsp. sour cream.

Old Drovers Inn Key Lime Pie
Makes two 10-inch pies.
Graham cracker Crust for two pies:
1/2 box Graham crackers
3 oz. butter
1 C. sugar
cinnamon and nutmeg to taste
Press mixture into two 10-inch glass pie plates and refrigerate while you prepare the filling.
Filling:
Grated peel of one lime
1 C. lime juice
8 egg yolks
2 cans of unsweetened condensed milk (Magnolia Brand works best.)
Combine and pour into crusts and refrigerate for at least six hours.

House & Garden printed a six page section on my prerevolutionary mill house in February 1968. The title was "Cheerfully Unconventional, A House to Delight the Senses and Comfort the Spirit." The story about the house was beautifully written and it explains my feeling so well I thought I would share some of it with you. Pratt Williams was the editor who did the sitting and the pictures were taken by Grisby. These same pictures and others that he took during the three days he photographed have been used in *English House and Garden* twice, *Casa Vogue, Maison and Jardin* and several other publications owned by Conde Nast.

I quote from the article, written by Elaine Greene:

"An appreciative guest once summed up the character of Kathryne Hays' 300-year-old remodeled mill in Roxbury, Conn., when she told her hostess, 'This house seems to embrace you.' Miss Hays, whose city life includes a New York apartment and a job as fashion editor of *Vogue*, was extremely pleased. Having worked painstakingly to create an environment that would delight the senses and comfort the spirit, she felt the house would have fulfilled her intentions if it turned out to be above all else a place where you feel loved.

"Her love for the house, in turn, is apparent in every delightful corner. It would take, literally, days of exploration for a visitor to examine and enjoy every detail that contributes to the consistent atmosphere that pervades the house, and days longer to learn where each object came from. Miss Hays is an insatiable collector who rummages with equal enthusiasm through the stocks of serious antiquarians and the scruffiest junk shops, and she has kept her eyes open in something like eighty countries. It's design that's important to me, not use or origin or monetary value, she says. And her collections cover so many different fields that you are reduced to saying that she collects the works of man. Then, wandering around the carefully tended gardens, noting the provisions made for the sustenance of birds and wild animals, finding under almost every big tree a chair of a different sort tucked away for savoring privately the varied aspects of the brook-fed valley, you have to add: The works of nature as well.

"An infinite capacity for taking pains, the familiar description of genius, aptly describes Miss Hays' way with a house. At home she is never idle: There is always a patch of brick paving she is working on, or a newfound bee box to be refinished, and no detail is too small for her attention. Not only is she concerned with the visual and tactile — among the feasts for the eye that she arranges are many you feel you must touch — but her house is seasoned with lovely things to listen to and sniff at. She augments the constant natural music of her eight waterfalls with bells and wind chimes — at a doorway, in a tree — and although she coaxes all the local songbirds to her property, she also has a housewide hi-fi system that can be switched outdoors. Everything she does is part of her environmental scheme and on her own imaginative terms, free from anyone else's rules - whether on furniture arrangement, color juxtaposition, or early Americana.

"The outdoors are as much a part of the all-embracing environment as the interior of Kathryne Hays' house, and her gardening is as imaginative and painstaking as the way she has furnished her rooms. She plans for all seasons, planting spring-time honeysuckle near autumn bittersweet, for instance, and her generous hand - when she put in flowering trees, she put in fifty — assures the effect. Sculpture is placed around the big natural swimming pool, and like sculpture, old chairs sit under the trees and old wagons and sleds dot the lawns.

"Privacy, which is as dear to Miss Hays as good design, is partly a component of the setting, for her house stands alone in a small valley and faces wild woodlands on three sides. With a firmly locked gate at the top of the steep steps leading from the roadside parking to the kitchen door, Miss Hays, who loves invited guests, but not drop-ins, can count on being serenely undisturbed.

"The old kitchen is where most people enter the house, and its very air is marvelous, fragrant with cinnamon sticks massed like pencils in a jar, pomander balls, drying apples, and flowers that have been grown, dried, and arranged by Miss Hays.

"When she remodeled the kitchen, she turned the major part of it into a dining room which includes the big cooking fireplace surrounded by a paneled wall. At the far end of the old kitchen she built a compact modern kitchen. Some guests linger an hour or more at the old plank table in the dining room, sipping coffee, inspecting the wall of tools, soaking up the atmosphere. But even if they pass through this room quickly, they know they are in a very special house where great care has been taken to please."

I agreed to let *House & Garden* photograph the house, but I did not feel it would be published. No two chairs match, I have no couch in the living room. It didn't seem like their style of house; it's much too personal.

The cost of the house and the twenty-five acres that came with it left me low on funds. I furnished it from country auctions, junk yards, antique shops, tag sales — any place I could find furniture that pleased me, fit within my budget, and was well designed.

My pieces of furniture were refinished and upholstered by me, something I had not done until necessity demanded that I do it.

The article seemed to make an impression on people. I received more than a thousand letters. They were mailed to me at the *Vogue* and Roxbury addresses. I do not know how many letters *House & Garden* received. The letters were kind, amusing, filled with questions and several impossible requests such as: "Please give me the plans and dimensions of the double bed with steps."

I didn't have the time to answer this mail and I had no plans. I had drawn a sketch of the bed, hired a cabinet maker to take the measurements of where the bed would sit, and make it. He hadn't made anything so large before, but he agreed to take the job. The bed was made in his cellar, and when it was completed, he found he couldn't get it out of the cellar, so he removed his steps in order to do so.

An antique dealer from North Carolina phoned my office. I was not there at the time, so he offered to pay for the call if I would return it. He offered me thirty thousand dollars for the old French metal table that was shown in the picture of my studio. He would also be glad to tell me its history. The call was not returned. I didn't have the nerve to tell him that the metal table is a strainer from a dairy that I bought at an auction because I liked its design, cut off the metal pipes, turned it upside down and it became a table. The cost to me was fourteen dollars.

The transition from mill to house was begun when I first saw it. Hobe Irwin had bought it, spent three years on the restoration. He did wonderful things that a woman would not have done. He brought large granite stones from the Roxbury quarry to be used as hearths for the fireplaces and as stoops for the front and side doors. He also put new brick into the chimneys, rewired the house and put in a new water system. The landscaping of the yard was exciting and pleasing to the eye. He had, through the use of walls and the natural valley, made the yard on five levels. The stream was rerouted and made into a large natural pool with a granite bottom. Two dams were built: a four foot dam going into the acre-size pool and a twenty foot dam at the other end. This permitted water to fall over the dam onto the fish steps and then continue down stream. There are eight small natural waterfalls, each with its own pool, before the first dam. The pool can be opened, emptied and cleaned.

It all seemed wonderful. True, the flood of 1955 had ruined the pool, but my real estate agent explained that was a small matter. Little did he know. The restoration wasn't finished, a new roof was needed, the top floor hadn't been started. There were no gardens, no storm windows (I later had forty-three installed). The list was unending and

I knew it would cost a lot of money, but no one could have talked me out of buying this house. It had my name on it and I knew I must have it. "Mr. Blandings and His Dream House" had little on me.

Everything I touched cost a thousand dollars. It took cranes and bulldozers two weeks to restore the pool. The franklin stove in the bedroom didn't work, so I removed it and reinstated the fireplace — it also didn't work. After seven different authorities were unable to make it work, I decided that I must learn to do things myself. I tried raising the floor of the fireplace by cementing in old tiles I had found in the yard. It smoked less, and I added another thickness, then another. It now works beautifully and I use the fireplace every night in the winter and often in the summer. It gets cool, due to the water and elevation, after nine in the evening.

I suffered through so much and my friends did the same. They helped paint, lay brick for terraces, build retaining walls for the stream, cut wood, and anything else that needed doing. The house needed painting, but I didn't want it shiny. I bought red barn paint, mixed it with lamp black and beryllium blue. After I got the right color I added large amounts of linseed oil. The combination worked like a dream. It was soaked up by the old siding boards and hasn't needed a coat of paint since, more than 30 years, except for the drainpipes and small details. Ignorance and common sense sometimes work better than knowledge or experience.

The work on the house drove me up the wall at times, but it also helped me keep my sanity. Someone, I wish I knew who, said, "Life is Maintenance." Since I bought this house I have spent four nights in the city and three in the country. I leave New York on Friday about one p.m. and return on Monday morning. I wait until my office opens so I can go over the day, and the week, with Kady on the phone. Then I drive to New York. This allows me to avoid the traffic, cut down on driving time and get the job started while I make the trip.

More than once I have arrived in Roxbury emotionally spent, so annoyed with something or someone that I was ready to "throw in the towel." Soon after I started working in my garden or arranging the table for dinner or placing fruit and flowers throughout the house, the tensions slipped away. The change of environment is wonderful. I never seem to get enough of either the country or the city. When time comes to leave I long for more time in each place.

Bill Gibbens and Doug Spingler owned a charming restaurant in Washington, Connecticut, just five miles from my mill, called "Today's." Going to their place for food was a treat. They had charming little touches that added so much to the enjoyment of the meal such as: A sprinkle of pumpkin pie spice added to the coffee, white wine in the quiche crust, mint pea soup, cucumber dill bisque, a chicken aspic served with green grapes, fresh pineapple and green grapes with a tablespoon of pear brandy, poached salmon with sorrel hollandaise, quenelles of chicken with tarragon mushroom sauce, apple vichyssoise.

Both men spent time in the theater. Doug said, "I was in more bombs than I can ever tell you. I always wanted to do my own thing. In the theater you depend on other people's personalities. My hobby was cooking. Cooking well isn't something that just comes out of the air. The basic thing is organization. You stage manage the party or the dinner. You cast your guests, your helpers."

While Doug and Bill lived in Washington they did a superb job of catering a number of dinner parties for me. I asked them if they would give me several menus and recipes for this book. I have listed them below:

> *Striped bass*
> *Braise sauce mousseline*
> *Carre d'agneau Bouquetiere*
> *Salade composee*
> *Plateau de fromages*
> *Souffle glace aux fraises*
> *Cafe*
> *Petit four*
>
> *Holiday Buffet Menu*
> *Cruditie*
> *Shrimp in beer batter*
> *Potato Skins*

Stuffed Mushrooms and Onion Sandwiches
Chinese Lemon Chicken
Blanquette de Veau
Rice — Salad
Bushe de Noel
Fresh Fruit Salad

Dinner Menu
Smoked Salmon
Fish Consomme
Parmesan profiteroles
Roast Veal (studded with proscuitto)
Spinach crepes
Broiled Tomatoes
Chateau Potatoes
Salad — Brie — Bread
Cranberry Cassis Mousse
Cookies

Luncheon Menu
Sweet Potato Chips
Chicken Spinach Souffle
Crepes with Butter Sauce
Broiled Tomatoes
Fresh Beet and Walnut Salad
Brie
Pepper-Herb Bread
Persian Quinces

Chicken and Spinach Souffled Crepes
4 skinned and boned chicken breasts cut into 16 strips
12 to 16 crepes (recipe follows)
spinach souffle
butter sauce

Crepes

4 eggs
1 cup water
2 cups "Wondra" flour
1/2 tsp. salt
2 T. oil or melted butter
2 T. dill, chives

Put first 3 ingredients in blender for 30 seconds. Add flour and blend for at least 1 minute. Add the rest of the ingredients and blend another 30 seconds.

Heat a 10 inch "non-stick" skillet to "hot-to-touch." Brush with small amount of oil. Pour a little less than 1/4 cup of batter, tilting the pan to coat the cooking surface. Cook until lightly browned on the bottom (1 to 1 1/2 minutes). Flip the crepe and cook an additional 30 seconds more. Remove crepe and place on a sheet of wax paper. Repeat process (brushing on a little oil when necessary) until all batter is used, continue placing waxpaper between each sheet. When finished, crepes can be wrapped and refrigerated up to 3 days. (Let crepes return to room temperature before continuing recipe.)

Spinach Souffle
4 T. flour
1/4 C. milk
3/4 C. scalded milk
5 eggs, separated
1 C. spinach (cooked, chopped, well-drained)
1/2 C. freshly grated parmesan cheese
salt
pepper
nutmeg

In a small bowl combine 4 T. flour with 1/4 C. milk, making a paste. Scald the 3/4 C. milk in a heavy saucepan, stirring in the paste mixture. Continue stirring until mixture is thickened. Add 4 egg yolks, one at a time, beating well after each yolk. Remove from heat.

Heat chopped spinach in one T. butter until warm. Combine the heated spinach and the above mixture. Add the parmesan cheese and season the spinach mixture with salt, pepper and nutmeg.

In a mixing bowl, beat the 5 egg whites with a pinch of salt, beating until they form stiff peaks. Fold 1/4 of the beaten whites into the spinach mixture to lighten the mixture. Then, gently fold the remaining egg whites to the mixture until well blended.

The Assembly:
16 crepes
16 chicken strips
spinach souffle
large oven-proofed dish, buttered

Place a crepe on a flat working surface. Put 1/4 C. of the souffle misture in the center of the crepe. Add a chicken strip and fold over the crepe, placing it in the buttered baking dish with the seam side down. Repeat until all crepes are filled and folded (two baking dishes may be needed). Bake in a preheated 375 degree oven for 30 to 35 minutes until center crepes are firm and well puffed.

While crepes are baking, make the following Butter Sauce:

Butter Sauce
2 C. milk
3 T. flour
3 T. unsalted butter
juice of 1 lemon
1 1/2 sticks unsalted butter (softened)

salt & pepper to taste

Heat milk in a saucepan. While the milk is heating, melt 3 T. butter in a non-aluminum sauce pan adding the flour and cook for 3 minutes, stirring frequently so the mixture does not burn. Remove from heat and add the warm milk. Whisk to blend and return to heat, continuing to wisk until well blended and thickened. Remove again from heat and add the 1 1/2 sticks of butter in small amounts, blending after each addition. After the butter is blended, add the lemon juice and salt and pepper to taste. (Sauce can be made ahead and re-heated in a double boiler.)

When crepes are baked, remove and pour 1/2 of the Butter Sauce over the crepes. Serve the rest of the sauce with the crepes at the table or buffet.

Beet-Walnut Salade

Place 1/4 lb. English walnuts on a cookie sheet in a 350 degree oven 10 - 15 minutes to brown. Cook, peel and quarter 1 lb. beets. In a small bowl or blender combine 2 T. red wine vinegar and 1/2 tsp. Dijon mustard and add 1/4 C. walnut oil in a stream, beating until well combined. Add salt and pepper to taste. In a salad bowl combine 1 small head Romaine, 1 head Bibb, the beets and toss with dressing. Sprinkle salad with walnuts.

Persian Quinces

Peel 4 quinces, place in deep baking dish. Drizzle 1/3 C. honey over them. Add 1 1/2 C. each of dry white wine and water, a 3-inch strip each of lemon peel and orange peel and a cinnamon stick. Cover dish tightly with foil and bake in 200 degree oven for 10 hours or longer until quinces turn pale (Persian) red and tender. With slotted spoon remove them to serving dish and strain sauce into small saucepan. Reduce syrup to 1 1/4 C., adding more honey if a sweeter syrup is desired.

This 10 hour process is a very old-fashioned procedure that was used when you had your kitchen stove going all the time to keep the kitchen warm. In the event you don't have a country kitchen to keep warm here is a more modern way to cook your quinces:

Peel, core and quarter the quinces and place them in a medium size, non-aluminum sauce pan. Add the honey, wine, water, citrus peel and cinnamon sticks. Heat to boiling and reduce heat to a simmer. Cover the pot and simmer until tender. (Approximately 30 to 45 minutes.)

Dugan, a fine Kerry Blue Terrier born on St. Patrick's day, came into my life two weeks after Shamus, my constant loving companion for fifteen years, had to be put down on Saturday before Easter, 1986. I knew Shamus was on his last year, but one is never fully prepared to give up one's pet. We were friends; we understood each other; we had respect for one another.

Even though I was devastated over my loss, I knew I must get another dog immediately. Mrs. Ruth Gettings, of Staten Island, a famous breeder of Kerry Blue Terriers and I had been in contact for over a year. Her dogs were well known for their dispositions as well as for their conformation. She did not have puppies at this time but set about to find me a dog descended from her kennel. The only dog a year or under was owned by Priscilla Schwenks, a breeder from Hershey, Penn. She had two, a year old female Kathleen and the male Dugan, but she wanted to show them and would not sell.

After numerous conversations, I finally prevailed upon Pricilla to part with Dugan.

My assistant, Kady, gave Dugan a rubber dog and he became so attached to the toy that he took it to his room, the kitchen, when I put him to bed. He was like Linus with his security blanket. One night soon after I brought him home, I awakened and noticed that the light was on in the kitchen, which seemed unlikely, since it was a ceiling light too high for a dog to reach. I got out of bed, went to the kitchen and found Dugan sitting happily in front of the refrigerator. The door was wide open and he was playing with his toy. He had not bothered the chicken or other food in the refrigerator. Instead he had figured out a way to open the door and used it as a night light so he could continue playing with his dog.

Dugan seems to be teaching me more than I teach him. I drove all the way to Hershey, Penn., a five hour trip each way, to get him. One of the most important things I learned from him was that regardless of the time and difficulty, he seems to improvise, to figure out a way to get the job done. I was playing ball with him for a long period of time and he always caught the ball and brought it back. Finally I had enough so I took the ball away and turned on the T.V. to see the Yankee game. Almost immediately he shifted his attention to the tube and each time a player hit a ball into center field darling Dugan ran wildly down the hall and waited to catch the ball.

Needless to say, I am enchanted with Dugan. He is bright, expressive, self-contained, inventive, and oh, so loving. He is like my shadow. When I take a step, he is with me. When I sit he sits, always so he can see my face. The best trait he possesses is his perpetual happiness. He listens to my every word and his tail wags with delight at my jokes, my stories and even at my routine comments. What an audience.

I rather enjoy the traveling that my job requires. The day after Labor Day I must leave for the Bologna shoe show and then from Italy I go to London for three days and Claridge's and then back to New York, but I find it almost impossible to leave my handsome four-legged cheerleader, Dugan.

I take the suitcases out at least a week before it is time to pack, so he won't go into a decline when he sees them.

Come January 21st I will be sixty-five and I can retire if I feel I would like to do so. There are so many things I want to do: Take a first class Pan American flight around the world; go on the great train from Chicago to Oregon so I can see the Rockies, the Tetons and the Northern U.S.; fly to San Francisco, drive through the country and then drive on to San Diego and fly back to N.Y. But how can I leave Dugan?

Once there was an excellent kennel in Roxbury called South-down, but it is no longer in business. When I went to Block Island this summer, Peg, my housekeeper, moved into my home and she and Dugan enjoyed their own vacation. When I go to Italy he will stay at the N.Y. apartment and Kady O'Connell, my assistant, will take care of him. At night she will take him to her apartment just a block away, but he will spend the day in his own home with frequent visits and walks from Kady and other friends.

Everyone tells me that it would be a mistake to retire, but I'm not so sure. I have worked for more than forty-five years, thirty-six of them as a fashion editor at *Vogue*. I'm tired of the stress, and I must think of the quality of my life. I need more time to just be me, expand my personal horizons, relax, inhale the stress free air, smell the roses.

I wonder if we make a mistake teaching our children to feel guilty if they don't work, or to make women fear middle age, to be frightened of loneliness, just being alone.

I would like to enjoy the pleasure and joys that come from having reached a certain age. Thanksgiving, was, and is, a family time. This year I saw young mothers and grandmothers who seemed more sure of themselves, more appealing, more beautiful and exciting than their children.

It made me think how sad it is to squander middle age, and dread its arrival when actually it is a precious luxurious time. A time when too much striving and ambition have given way to the inner search, not to the exclusion of rejecting outside happenings, activities, stimuli, or compelling work, but rather including the sweet tender sound of silence.

It's taking time to look deeply into the eyes of a friend to see if all is well, listening to the timbre of his voice, seeing.

It takes a certain seasoned maturity to realize that the struggle for security is a fruitless and sightless search, and like quick silver is difficult to hold on to, and often suffocatingly dull when held.

How beautiful and satisfying it is to find oneself, and even more rewarding to like what is found. There is a special nobility that comes with middle age. It's the best time of life, a time when it's all there for the taking. What is so precious is the aesthetic pleasure that comes from sharing, helping, giving — and having the sense and sensibility to do so with grace.

It is refreshing and fulfilling to know someone with a generous spirit that any well spent number of years can bring. It's an age (the number of years is not important) when there is more available time because one has learned to let go of the needless frustrations that are time consuming and energy wasting.

Middle age isn't the dark side of the moon, but rather the irresistible pulsating time when experience should shut out the deadly demons of doubt and frustration.

So many people, especially women, tend to dread (and sometimes spoil because of the dread) a time when the years have been the condiments that brought to life tang, spice, spontaneity, and focus.

I would like to shout from the highest peak and say to the many who are uptight about approaching years, "Don't be afraid of menopause, the children growing up leaving an empty house, life without a husband, celebrating your fiftieth birthday, feeling useless. It's all there for the taking or perhaps I should say, the making. Passion and desire do not wear out. The spirit is inexhaustible; the romance with life is just beginning."

Each Friday I pack the car, mainly with food. I keep clothes in the country, so I will not need to take them back and forth. Peg shops for the basics, but I take New York's special food with me. First I go to Harry, Stanley and Allen of Green Valley Foods on First Avenue and 50th. They have freshly cooked chicken waiting for me, also daily fresh eggs from New Jersey farms. They wrap chicken in aluminum foil so it is still hot when I reach my mill two hours later. I go to the Koreans for the finest fruits and vegetables, the Artichoke for bread and salads.

Since I got arthritis I have tried every diet possible hoping something will help. It may not work for everyone but since I gave up certain foods the arthritis has improved tremendously. I eat no red meat. Instead, I'm happy with chicken and fish. I do not eat shellfish except lobster and shrimp. Other foods I have eliminated are spinach, liver and other organ meats, tomatoes, potatoes, green pepper, eggplant. Also I exercise every day. Swimming did wonders for me. Each day I swam a little farther until I found I could swim a mile without stopping, 125 laps at the health club pool. I must admit I do not now swim each day, but I do exercise in my home, as well as walk the dog. While I did swim I felt on a high when I left the health club, but found that I was too tired by the evening time. Instead of going to business dinners I wanted to go to bed. Also I disliked swimming when the weather was too cold or in the heat of summer, and it took at least an hour and a half of my time.

Dugan was not an experienced car traveler. He was taken to a show placed in a cage in a van. When I took him from his home in Hershey he was placed on the back seat by himself. As we drove away he stood on his back legs, looked out the rear window and whimpered just once. I felt worse than he did. It was a sweet and sad moment. I hoped he would be happy with me and that he wouldn't miss his family too much.

Oddly enough, except for the very beginning, he responded well to his new environment, to getting all the attention, rather than having to compete with his mother, father, and sister. We became a family rather quietly and he never cried at night or during the day when I was at work. For several months I came home at some time around lunch to feed and walk him.

Animals are terribly important to people of all ages who live alone, and today there are many people who do. Also I have worked with older people confined to a home or hospital and the presence of an animal, even for a visit is invaluable. It's someone to touch, to give and receive affection.

One darling little 84 year old lady said, "I can't remember when I was last kissed. When this puppy licked my face it made me feel loved again." Also I think an animal helps keep one from getting old. You must stay healthy and active in order to look after the pet and somehow one measures up to the responsibility and enriches her life by sharing it with a living, breathing creature who needs her.

A friend regularly visited two older ladies in a home. She noticed that one of them named Ethel seemed to be more depressed and less interested in her surroundings on each visit. She sat and asked Ethel what she could do for her. Ethel at this time was 92, and she wept and said she wanted her mother. The next time my friend visited she took a baby kitten with her. It wasn't easy to do so, but she got permission to give the kitten to the ladies. They were enchanted. They perked up almost immediately and loved and cared for the pet with all the tenderness that they needed to share. The ladies and the kitten had many happy months together. They had a reason to get out of bed, to move, to communicate.

Roxbury House in reflection

Kay's Bedroom in Roxbury House

Kathryne Hays

Roxbury House in snow

Terrace outside of Roxbury House

Guest Bedroom in Roxbury House

Top Floor of Roxbury House

Dugan

Dining Room of Roxbury House

Living Room of Roxbury House

A Good Time
Was Had By All

There are hundreds of formulas for giving a party. Some good, some better, but in my book the best parties, like sex, are in the head and the heart. People have a good time when they feel wanted, desired, and welcome, and the house is warm and inviting. In some countries one is greeted by the hostess saying "My house is your house." I like to say to a new guest who comes to my mill, "My house embraces you." And I always hope it does.

Someone said the essence of a good dinner party is that half the guests should be invited to impress and the other half should be there to be impressed. That's not my formula. I do feel, however, that the mix is of first importance and then the food. The guest list should be made up of compatible, interesting doers who enjoy listening and who have the desire to share good conversation without the need to dominate. I enjoy guests who have a light touch, who are glad they came and who left home with the intention of having a lovely evening.

My favorite size dinner party is usually 10 to 12 people. It is not necessary that the sexes be equally divided. I consider that old-fashioned. Today there are more women than men, so why invite a dud just because he is a man or because she is a woman. I invite individuals not sexes.

I like to plan a party well in advance. My friends tease me about the napkins getting dusty because I set the table so early — not true.

A young person asked for a few simple tips for a country dinner for 10. These are the ones that come to me first:

Champagne sitting in the snow outside the door to the dining room is appealing and gay. It gives a festive air to the evening.

A large generous fire in one or more rooms where the guest will be sitting.

An ample amount of oversized, lit candles. I especially like the ones that need no candle holders.

A relaxed hostess who enjoys her own party. The evening should be original with wit and adventure.

A tranquil and lovely countryside helps give atmosphere to the evening.

166

Animals who move freely through the house adding to the delight of rural charm, and bring warmth to the occasion.

I prefer good company, good food, good wine to formality. A good salad is essential to a good meal and mixing it is an art. Do not toss; instead, use a gentle hand and fold like eggs. I like using nasturtiums, violets, sageflowers or rose petals added after the salad is mixed. Try salads with no lettuce.

I like a vegetable course slightly cooked so the vegetables are still crisp.

The Hurlbut farm in Roxbury is famous for its many varieties of corn, apples, and berries in season. I use them as well as their pumpkins and squash. Two especially delicious corn varieties are Silver Queen and Butter & Sugar (part white, part yellow).

They grow many types of apples. When the Danbury fair was still running every year, they were known for winning first prize for their numbers of different apples. Several of these are Pipin, Macintosh, Golden Delicious, Red Delicious, Cortland, Macoun.

Because I think of calories, I cook with herbs and with wine and use almost no butter. My dining room is the original mill kitchen with a walk-in cooking fireplace. It is the first room you enter, so it becomes the focal point of the house — a place to congregate, communicate, to enjoy and linger. I have collected, over the years, oversized antique cooking utensils and hung them on the paneled wall. This adds an informal quality to the room. I made a modern kitchen but it's the old kitchen where guests sit and relax before the fire. It's a meeting room.

Unless I have good help, I stick to food that does not demand my undivided attention. I cook things that can be prepared well in advance. When I was growing up, even though we had help, my mother was always exhausted after a party. I felt that the guests would have preferred to spend more time with her during the evening. A meal should have style, but it can be a relaxed style.

There are times when the simpler the meal, the better the food. Even a one item dinner can work beautifully, especially if the wine is superb, and there is fresh fruit for dessert. Two one-course meals that come to mind are the following:

1/2 butternut squash for each person. I cut the squash in half, score out the seeds, put on salt and pepper, place in tight heavy aluminum foil and cook for an hour in a hot oven (or until a fork enters easily). When brought from the oven, I add butter, brown sugar (or Equal) and grate fresh nutmeg over the entire squash. A second good one-course meal is new fresh baby potatoes, cooked with their peeling on and topped with butter, chives or sour cream and chives.

Since I must think of my diet I celebrate the meal, the occasion as much as the food.

No evening meal seems complete to me without an assortment of good cheeses, hard as well as soft, and freshly ground coffee. I like to grind the coffee at the last minute so the aroma fills the room. After coffee I have a selection of brandies or cognac for those who enjoy them. They are served on a tray so the guest can select their favorite.

Whenever possible I like to send guests home with a portion of cake or freshly baked loaf of bread to enjoy with their breakfast.

Kathleen O'Connell, a good Irish name, has been with me at *Vogue* for more than eighteen years. I hired her at the age of 19 when she graduated from the Fashion Institute of Technology. She is an excellent cook who specializes in tasty dishes loaded with calories, especially her desserts. I asked her to give me several typical Irish recipes. These are some favorites:

Corned Beef and Cabbage

My rule of thumb for corned beef is always buy too much so the leftovers can be used for delicious sandwiches and savory hash. Place the meat in a large kettle of simmering water containing a peeled onion imbedded with 10 peppercorns. Since most corned beef is too salty, after twenty minutes of cooking drain the meat and return to another kettle of simmering water. If put back into cold water the meat will toughen. After one hour test with a fork. It is done when tender. Let it stand in liquid for twenty minutes before cutting.

Serve with quartered cabbage and thick chunks of carrots that have been cooked in the meat broth, tiny steamed red potatoes, red horseradish (horseradish and beets), or mustard for purists, and plenty of Harp beer.

Irish Soda Bread
Beat together:
2 C. buttermilk
1 egg
2 1/2 C. flour
1/4 tsp. baking soda
1 tsp. salt
1/2 C. caraway seeds
1 - 1 1/2 C. raisins
1 T. plus 1 tsp. baking powder
1/2 C. sugar

Blend all ingredients together. Pour into a greased and floured loaf pan, bake at 375 degrees for 1 hour and 15 minutes.

Apple Sauce Cake
1 C. butter
2 C. sugar
2 eggs
2 1/2 C. flour
1/2 tsp. salt
2 tsp. baking soda
1 tsp. cinnamon
1 tsp. cloves
2 C. raisins
2 C. chopped nuts
2 C. hot apple sauce

This recipe requires a very strong mixer or arm. Cream butter and sugar gradually until smooth and creamy. Add the well beaten eggs and blend well. Mix and sift all dry ingredients. Add to the first mixture and mix well, then add raisins and nuts, after blending well add hot apple sauce. Turn into a well greased loaf or tube pan and bake at 350 degrees for 1 hour and 15 minutes or until a toothpick inserted in middle comes out clean.

Sauerkraut and Dumplings
Roast two thick pork chops per person in a shallow pan with a large chopped onion tossed into pan and sprinkling of salt and pepper. When tender, make a brown gravy with pan drippings. Drain two large cans of sauerkraut after rinsing in cold water. Simmer the kraut for one hour, then add one grated peeled potato to thicken and cook for fifteen minutes more, adding half a cup of pan gravy. Bring a large covered kettle of water to a boil for your dumplings:

3 C. flour
2 eggs
3/4 C. water
1/2 tsp. baking powder
1/2 tsp. salt
Beat eggs in water. Add to mixed and sifted dry ingredients.

Dough will be very sticky. Drop in generous spoonfuls into boiling water. Keep pot covered for three minutes, uncovered for remaining seventeen. Test by cutting one open. They should have a dry texture in the middle. Serve the kraut spooned over the dumplings. Left over dumplings are delicious sliced and sauteed in butter and served with scrambled eggs.

Egg Nog Pie

A rich and satisfying dessert, especially in the winter, is Egg Nog Pie: Use regular graham crumb crust. Beat six egg yolks until light and add 1 scant cup sugar. Soak one envelope, 1 T. gelatin in 1/2 C. cold water until dissolved. Put the gelatin and water over low flame, bring it to a boil and pour while hot over the sugar-egg mixture stirring briskly. Whip 1 pint of heavy cream until stiff. Fold it into the egg mixture and flavor with 1/2 C. dark rum. Cool until the mixture begins to set and pour into the pie shell. Chill until firm. Sprinkle the top of the pie generously with shaved bittersweet chocolate curls.

Each party needs beautiful flowers throughout the house. The flowers play an important part in setting the mood of the evening. When my garden is in bloom I prefer using flowers from it. One of the most glorious and rewarding category of flowers is the lily. It is often brilliant or white, always delicate and has a dignified beauty. Lilies do well in a leafy garden, which I have. They are handsome plants with promise. They add grace and charm to the garden and are great cut flowers for entertaining. Two of the easiest and most noble lilies are the Japanese lily and the tiger lily. The Japanese, some call them Bermuda lilies because they grow so well in Bermuda, can live happily among quiet greenery or even as a potted plant that becomes easy to take into the house for special occasions. Not only are lilies beautiful, but they have body and stature so they easily fill a spot that needs a tall and dramatic plant.

Soon after I bought the old mill I stocked my streams with rainbow trout. I do not enjoy catching fish, or any animal, but a large number of my friends get a glazed look in their eyes at the thought of fishing, and my property has a generous amount of fat juicy worms for those who fish with worms.

Francois Ilnseher, a lovely and talented hairdresser and friend, fished on his free time when we photographed, several times, for *Vogue* at my mill and in the village of Roxbury. When I first met Francois he was a hairdresser at Kenneth's Salon in New York City.

Kenneth lives a few doors from me on Beekman Place, and we talk almost every day when we walk our dogs. He's an attractive, up man who makes me feel good just knowing him. Dugan had just been groomed when we met Kenneth. He laughed and said, "I believe I can still recognize a new haircut, Dugan." Our dogs are not yet too friendly. Kenneth's beautiful Schitz-zu Tiger is willing but Dugan isn't yet agreeable. Francois caught many trout, as did other friends, so we put those not needed at the time in the freezer.

At one time I had more than 35 nice-sized frozen rainbows. It seemed a good idea to have a dinner party and invite those who had caught the trout. At the time I had a broken leg that was in a cast and didn't feel I could handle the party myself so I called a neighborhood French restaurant in the country to ask if they would use my trout for a dinner. They agreed and we had a charming trout party.

There are those who fry trout, but I like it best when it is cooked in the oven. I put lemon and parsley on the fish; tightly wrap it in aluminum foil and let it stay in a hot oven for a short period of time (about 10 minutes). It's delicious, with all its natural flavor.

Since my background is so interwoven with the Deep South, I made a list of typical southern foods:

Baby Lima Beans with Bacon
Wild Rice with Vegetables or with Oysters
Spoon Bread made with Cornmeal
Corn Pudding
Hot Biscuits
Baked Grits
Black-eyed Peas cooked with a Ham Hock
Mustard Greens
Rainbow Trout Almandine
Chicken with Orange Sauce served with Yams
Chicken Dijon
Southern Fried Chicken
Chicken with Peaches
Cornish Hens with grape Cognac
Shrimp Pate, Chicken Liver Pate
Turkey stuffed with Cornbread, Oysters and Pecans

or with Apples and Chestnuts
Pork stuffed with Prunes
Pork with Orange Sauce
Candied Yams
Hot Potato Salad
Floating Island with Berries
Sweet Potato Pie
Peach Cobbler with homemade Ice Cream
Pecan Pie
Blackberry Pie
Chilled Watermelon Balls with Mint
Lemon Cheesecake
Sliced Peaches with Grand Mariner
Fruit Cake with Blackberry Wine
Apple Sauce Cake with Fruits and Nuts

Dugan has cultivated a party taste. He is not given tid bits from the table or when we have cheese with drinks on the terrace, so he does not expect to share people food. From the beginning, I teach my dogs not to steal food when it is on a low table and this stays with them. Dugan has done real well; however, I noticed that whenever we have champagne he invariably takes a couple of licks from someone's glass.

I would like to quote a few paragraphs from a book that Jessica Daves wrote called, *Vogue's Book of Menus and Recipes*:

> "One mark of a good party is that the guests go away feeling more attractive than when they came. And the guest is more important than the menu, the flowers, the wine, or the service. To plan the guests well is the first move; it is fairly improbable that there will not be some people invited because of 'obligations'; but if all the guests are there for reasons of social debts, that fact hangs like a pall over the gathering. For a successful party there must be some free, attractive spirits who are invited simply because they are so attractive, and

who lift the amusement quotient by their presence. Also: Variety in ages is becoming more and more a facet of good parties: And guests with different interests are likely to make a more entertaining evening than, say, a whole company of stockbrokers or of dress designers or of college dons. But it is the hosts who set the tone; and thoughtful hosts have a way of making even dull guests glitter. All of us have felt it occasionally — the warm pleasure of having our special qualities appreciated and subtly presented to the company. The mere inviting of a guest is not enough for a memorable evening; he must be made to know that he is an asset to the party."

Also from the same book is a good suggestion concerning wine with the meal:

"Almost never, in any dinner except the really formal, is it necessary to serve more than one wine. Pleasant, yes, to serve a little sherry with the soup, a nice Chablis with the fish, and a good claret with the rest of the dinner. Champagne can be added for the dessert, but these are not really necessary for the perfection of the dinner. A famous and hospitable duchess serves these four wines almost invariably. But some good hostesses serve champagne only, using it as an aperitif, and serving it throughout the dinner. Certainly one good wine plus champagne is a good plan; but again, here we might paraphrase Pepys: Make sure that the wines are not only "noble, but enough." Nothing seems more inhospitable than a scanty serving of wines or wine of poor quality at a real dinner party."

House & Garden assembled a book on "Creative Entertaining." I was flattered that they used a picture of the living room in my mill for the chapter called, "The Hospitable House." I won't quote the entire thing, but only the last sentence:

> "To be truly hospitable is to share with others your own delight in living."

In the same book they say:

> "People aren't hung up any longer on the idea that you can't give a dinner party without a dining room. Or that a big bash is a bore. Or that you can't entertain with style in the kitchen. There are no more set rules that spell out what a party is to be — or where. The issue is, rather, what makes any party a great one? Whether it's a simple dinner for six, dancing for sixty, or an open house for twice that; your party will be memorable if you give it the best of yourself.
>
> > "Start with comfort...
> > Add delight...
> > Then bring in a surprise...
> > Make your aim diversion."

Since I have talked mainly about small parties, or parties connected with the home, I felt it would be remiss not to speak of a large commercial party.

The first person who came to mind as the best party giver around is Helen O'Hogan. Helen and I have been friends and have worked closely together during the more than 30 years that she has been at Saks Fifth Avenue. She is a vice-president in charge of Public Relations for, at last count, Saks' 44 stores, and has given well over 1000 parties in the capacity. I asked her if she would give me what she considers the most important ingredients that go into producing a large successful party. Even though Helen was lined up with wall-to-wall meetings and headed for three weeks at the European Collections, she very graciously took the time to write the following:

175

"During 1986 I planned a variety of large-scale parties which included the gala opening of three new stores, one seated dinner-dance, and the usual assortment of cocktail parties that accompany the large number of fashion shows which Saks Fifth Avenue sponsors each year. The people attending these parties numbered around 8,000.

"The season passed successfully without any major mishaps. Such is not always the case, however. Having been planning the parties for 38 store openings, I have gradually developed a fool proof system to pull off the 'perfect party.'

"The most important thing to do is PLAN IN ADVANCE. This is the best way to foresee and avoid any potential mishaps.

"No matter where the party is being planned, no matter what city, make sure you OBTAIN THE BEST CATERER in the area. Get references, menu suggestions, and if possible attend a party they have catered. During the preliminary stages of selecting, it is terribly important to meet and talk with the caterers individually to make sure the client / consultant chemistry is right. If the rapport isn't right when you begin, things will only get worse later on.

"DEVELOP A WORKABLE MENU. It doesn't matter whether the occasion is lavish or simple. The menu must work and must be different. For most of our two-hour long cocktail parties, we have found that a 'supper by the bite' menu works best."

"The SUPPER-BY-THE-BITE concept was developed by a caterer I used in 1978 in planning the gala opening of our store in Skokie, Illinois. It lends itself well to the traditional cocktail party, since all the items are finger foods. But at the same time the menu functions as a full course meal in miniature. Appetizers are all found in one location, entree type foods in another, and dessert and coffee in another. When our stores have three floors, we plan a different course on each level. By far, the most popular item is seafood. We set up a seafood bar filled with clams on the half shell, boiled jumbo shrimp, mussels, and sometimes crabmeat.

"The AMOUNT OF FOOD required is equally important. Nothing is worse, from the guests' point of view, than to leave feeling hungry. I always like to allow 14 to 17 pieces of food per person during a two hour party.

"SERVICE is frequently an area that is not given the kind of attention that it so richly deserves. I like to allow one waiter per 15 guests and one bartender for every three feet of bar. This may seem a bit extravagant, but if you keep in mind that servicing your guests is your number one priority, such care and attention is a must! Table linens must be of the highest quality and should touch the floor. Serving dishes and utensils are always the finest silver and glassware is always made of glass — never plastic. We also use bamboo and black lacquer for serving. I believe these requirements are so critical, I always ask for photos of the glassware, service and uniforms, plus linen samples.

"Uniforms for all service personnel are black tie, with the waitresses dressed in French maid uniforms — black dresses with white collar, cuffs and apron.

"Once you believe everything is set — but before you open the doors — make sure you DO A FINAL CHECK. While doing this at the gala party of our new Palm Springs store, I discovered that while the waitresses were wearing black dresses, (I had asked for black waitress uniforms with white collar and cuffs) the skirts were short mini-skirts worn with net stockings! Therefore, it was necessary for us to pull longer skirts from the store's existing inventory. During the final check of our Dallas store opening I discovered much to my dismay that the silver trays and chafing dishes which were being used were badly tarnished and dented. At the last minute, we had to rent new service equipment.

"The coat check operation for our Cincinnati opening went anything but smoothly. Having had the assurance of the caterer's personnel that they knew how to operate a coat check, we found, 45 minutes into the party, that instead of taking the coat check tickets in numerical order, they were simply pulling the first ticket they came to, causing the coat check to be in total disarray. The rest of the evening was spent in rehanging all the garments. Luckily we only lost one hat, which was found the next day.

"As a prospective host or hostess of one of these parties, you must realize that it is incumbent upon you to really know and care about food. STRIVE FOR VARIETY of presentation and insist upon it from your catering personnel. Developing an American style menu for our annual SFA/USA show might have seemed rather dull and uninteresting to some caterers. But Glorious Food fashioned a menu that was both simple and elegant.

"The menu began with a piquant corn chowder served with home-style cornbread, followed by roasted breast of chicken accompanied by a peppery barbecue sauce, pureed squash and tri-color cole slaw. The meal finished with an airy peanut mousse, coffee and liqueurs. It was a tremendous hit!

"It is important to spread your most distinguished guests around the room. The precise seating at these tables is quite another matter. Things are always changing. If there's a perfect way to seat a party, I'd like to know what it is.

"As you go about planning for the perfect party, it pays to plan for the worst thing that could possibly happen. By all means, plan for rain, and make sure you have everything necessary to cope with it if and when it happens — that means, obtaining canopies, carpet, umbrellas, whatever is needed.

"If there's one thing I've learned in all these years of planning parties, it is if something can go wrong, it will."

Delights

Life is made up of delights. To some it may be a sunset, wonderful sex, a good meal, an exciting trip, a new baby, a special car, buying a dream house, a promotion, beautiful music, a good show or just to touch the hand or look into the eyes of a special friend. What ever delights you most, life should be sprinkled with the warm loving rains of joyful doings.

I have always operated under the illusion that if you intertwine your days and nights with sparkling actions there will be little time and room for those downbeat empty feelings.

When I started living alone, after four years in college with a roommate and an immediate marriage, I found I was almost frightened to be by myself. It took me about three years to make peace with the real me — to find the real me, in order to be an effective human being, to live my own life and not to live through someone else. I worked on searching for the delicious side of living.

Many times I backslid and had pity for lonely me, but more often I became acquainted with the glorious side of my friends and myself.

Oddly enough it's necessary to find bubbling, dynamic people or one settles for the mundane, eighth carbon copy, passive type of person.

After my divorce, a friend from Bucks County, Penn., breeder of Kerry Blue Terriers, gave me a puppy for Christmas. Up to this time I had not owned a dog in the city, and felt it might be too difficult to do and go to my job each day. She explained that I must make my pick of the litter so she could sell the other pups. Another friend and I drove to Pennsylvania to bring home my new baby dog — and he was a baby, just under six weeks old. Since that first experience I have found that it is easier to get a terrier after three months of age, or even better at six months. A terrier is so wired, so high-strung, so foxy, he learns to take advantage at this extra young age, and the owner lets him because he is a baby. Once bad habits are formed, they are hard to break.

It was not until my second Kerry Blue fifteen years later that I felt equipped to handle this bright, demanding breed. The introduction of a dog into my city apartment wasn't easy, but it added a dimension and responsibility to my Manhattan life. I quit staying out so late. I gave more of myself and I found it necessary to go home every evening after work in order to feed and care for the dog. It didn't take long for this loving, giving dog to captivate me. He made big demands but the benefits outweighed all other considerations. I was hooked and haven't been without a dog since that day. With a little extra energy and attention a dog or cat can have a healthy, happy life in the city.

I wish I had the wisdom to write something noble and splendid that would add to the sense of well being to someone who is reaching out for a more fulfilled life. I wish I knew the answers, but mostly I feel I don't even know the questions. I feel frustrated that I am not better equipped to make an extraordinary time out of a disappointment, to help add pure joy and quality to the life of a loved one whose moment begs for lightness, a little tenderness and perhaps an original adventure.

The leaves are falling in the country, as well as on Beekman Place. Each time I walk Dugan my car is covered. I keep my car parked on the street in front of my Maisonette. Each year the trees on Beekman Place grow taller and stronger, have more branches and leaves. I wonder if people can stretch, add sympathetic understanding as the trees add new growth. Surely it must be possible.

Through the years I've wondered if I would run dry with ideas for my work. It hasn't happened. Now I wonder if the emotions run dry as we reach certain ages. Recently I came to the conclusion that it can't happen. One reaps what one sows, earns the beauty lines on the face and feels thankful for them. At least they show character.

November has blown into New York with a chilly breeze. It's refreshing after a beautiful mellow October. Dugan is frisky and alert. Dogs like the cold weather. It gives them, as it does us, a renewed vitality. They like to kick up their heels and run with the wind. New York has hot summers and cold winters; however, I like living in a place where the seasons change. It's more interesting; it keeps one awake, gives you a nudge now and then to keep moving, stay alert, seize the moment. On such a day as today I feel like a celebration, but too often that includes glorious foods, and my more than ample shape can't accommodate the calories.

One of the delights of my week is a glorious and charming little girl, Darvina Cohen. I call her my Jewish Princess. She lives in the same building that I live in on Beekman Place. She is beautiful, warm, sensitive and bright as a penny. It is not unusual in the morning when I go for my first walk with Dugan to find a work of art (drawn by my six year old Princess) slipped under the door of my private lobby. Darvina was fond of Shamus and quiet tears came to her eyes when her mother explained that Shamus was old and ill and would die before too long. I felt close to this darling, sensitive child when her mother explained death to her. She has the grace and humanity of a much older child. I cherish our friendship.

When I came home with Dugan, Darvina was one of his first new acquaintances. She drew me a scene for Shamus' death, and a lighter gayer one with balloons to welcome Dugan..

Halloween night I was tired and was taking an early nap when Willy, the building superintendent rang on the house phone to ask if the children might call on me. Because Dugan barks at the house phone I could not understand what he said, so I went out into the building lobby to get his message. Darvina was there, with her father. Two other beautiful little girls, Kathleen and Elizabeth, were also in the lobby with their mother Susan Leiderman. Susan and David own David's Cookies and a number of other enterprises. They live in a remodeled brownstone in the neighborhood. The three little girls were dressed in their mothers' clothes with make-up, jewelry, and Darvina even had on a hat.

Since the scare of pins in candy I don't buy food for the children; however, I save my change and give each a hand filled with pennys, dimes and nickels. Just as I was dividing the change, two small boys and their mother appeared. They were the sons of Frank Rich (drama critic of the New York Times) and his wife, who also live in the same building. Children all dressed in their world of fantasy are a special, amusing, and satisfying delight. The sound of happy children's voices is a gay and joyful sound and one that I cherish. On a day like Halloween they are light-hearted and their aliveness is contagious. Dugan rises to the occasion and joins in the fun with happy barks and tail waggings.

Tonight I stayed home to see the Women's Virginia Slims Championships tennis matches on television, but they came on late (10 p.m.). While I was filling in time for the tennis I listened to a celebration of George Gershwin on Channel 13. Music plays such an important role in my sense of well being. I can be flustered, confused, a little depressed and down, but good music well-presented makes everything right. It makes me light up like a firefly or soothes over the frustration and makes me feel quieted and smooth as cream.

When I married in 1942, the war was on and we needed to find an apartment where I could work at my job as a research chemist at DuPont in Arlington, N.J. and one where my husband (a signal corp. officer at Fort Monmouth) could commute on the weekends. Apartments weren't easy to find, and we wanted something attractive, and rather special for our first home. We settled for a captivating apartment that belonged to a Harvard professor, that was in upper Montclair, N.J. He used the apartment in the summer. It took some doing, but we persuaded him to rent it to us until the army allowed us to live near the post at Fort Monmouth.

I moved into this darling apartment several months before our wedding at the "Little Church Around the Corner" in New York City. One of the special delights of our new home-life together was a complete record collection of George Gershwin. We played the records so much they almost wore out. To this day, Gershwin is deep within my being. The music outlived the marriage, but both were good, and both added ginger to my life. George understood romance so well and yet he never married. Think how many people for whom he has set the stage and how many love affairs he has advanced, bless him! I don't usually envy anyone, but how I wish I could write and produce beautiful music. I play the harmonica, the piano, the guitar (all badly) but when I was young I sang folk songs reasonably well. Even though my voice isn't what it was as a girl, the music is still there in my soul. I remember the lyrics of most songs that I heard, especially the hymns that we sang at church when I was a girl.

This day, November 19, 1986, was the first real winter day. The night's hard rain washed away the leaves on Beekman Place and gave the streets a shiny clean face. When I took Dugan on his first morning outing at 6 a.m. the rain had stopped. The wind was strong and chilled and the morning was breathtakingly beautiful. At 6:15 the street lights go off, just before strong light, and cars covered with snow were moving about. N.J., Westchester and Conn. had several inches of snow during the night. Many people were left without lights.

The morning was so lively, it felt good to inhale deeply and to enjoy Dugan's animated reaction to the cold weather. I didn't phone Peg in Roxbury to see if all was well. I felt sure that she was looking after the house, and I didn't want to hear any disturbing news to spoil this sensuous morning. It made me feel that the best is yet to come — a special feeling indeed for one nearly 65 years of age.

Dugan and I stood in front of Irving Berlin's house at the end of 50th and Beekman Place, and watched the boats slide up and down the East River. The tankers looked like they were close enough to touch. We could have enjoyed this unusual scene for a longer period of time but there is a large German Shepherd dog who also walks at this hour. He and Dugan are less than friendly, so I try to keep them from meeting face to face. His owner is thoughtful; so if we try, we can co-exist nicely. It's funny what a strong and good impression a day like this can make on everyone. The doormen were arriving for their 7 a.m. change of duty. I am constantly surprised at how different they look in their own clothes, rather than in their uniforms. We wave silently to each other. At this early hour I try not to speak or let the dog bark for fear someone's sleep will be disturbed. Before Dugan, I was a late sleeper so I realize how prized the last hours of sleep are to those who rise at a less tender hour. Who knows, I may learn to love the sun-rising hour.

Another special sight most days on this famous little two-block street is Irving Berlin (about 97 years) who takes his walk almost every day with one of the doormen. He is spry and looks well — far younger than his years. Also many days one can see Garbo who lives on East 52nd Street but knows that she can walk undisturbed on Beekman Place.

When I first moved to New York one of the favorite plays that I saw was Laurette Taylor in Tennessee Williams' *Glass Menagerie*. To this day, hundreds of plays later, I still find it one of the best plays

I've seen. Laurette Taylor lived in a brownstone on Beekman Place in her earlier days, as did Katherine Cornell and Gutherie McKlintock — Paul Rudolf, the architect, now owns and occupies the house. I've lived here more than 30 years in my sweet Maisonette and even though I own my apartment, it's really the other way around. It's the street that owns the people. It takes them in, gives them its peace, security and protection or coughs them up and lets them go on their way.

This sparkling little street has its own magic and its own personality. It's somewhat haunted by the famous names that have lived here. The trees are dressed with blooming flowers around them except for deep winter when they are covered with ivy, and the brass on the doors is brightly polished. Each doorman wears a smile and calls many residents and their dogs by name. We have at least two doormen in our building who have been here more than 25 years. It's satisfying and comforting to see familiar faces through the years, very much like living in a small town, and yet here we are in mid-Manhattan.

This has been an unusually busy week due to next week's Thanksgiving closing. Anytime a holiday occurs it causes extra preparation and earlier release dates for *Vogue*'s pages.

Yesterday we had an editorial meeting until noon. I was expected at Maud Frison's new offices on East 56th to finally see her complete line. Due to time and gridlock I couldn't go out to lunch, so had a chicken salad while we worked. The shoe line was exceptionally good and filled with interest in color as well as design. Also it's a pleasure to work with Cookie, Maud's valuable assistant and the manager of her store.

Maud gave me a bright red dog collar she had made for Dugan, with his name. It had been made in Europe and had arrived that morning. After finishing her line we went into another office to see the new "Miss Maud" shoes that are handled by her attractive young daughter Sophie. I was pleased with the line and enjoyed meeting Sophie and a young French school companion who was working with her. It is like a breath of fresh air to work with these bright shiny young talents. They are blessed with enthusiasm, and a desire to be successful.

When Sophie was in school at New York University we had talked on the phone. She was having a little trouble with her weight, but no more. She now has a good lean shape and a special, captivating charm.

After Maud, I went to my next appointment with Wendy Newman at the new Prada shop on E. 57th just east of Madison Avenue. The shop is beautifully done and I wish them luck. Prada is better known in Europe than in the U.S.; however, time will change that.

Another appealing new salon that has opened recently is the Joan and David shop at 816 Madison Avenue. It is attractive and even more so when their darling white Bichon Frisee sits in the shop window. His name is Bijou, and he and I are special friends. When I arrive at their office to work, Bijou greets me with loud and friendly barks, and sits in a chair next to me while I look at the shoes.

Each year when I arrive in Bologna, Bijou is always watching for me, just as though he knew what time I would get there. Joan has her show room on the main floor of the hotel where I stay. Bijou hears my voice when I sign in and runs the entire length of the lobby to greet me. After a long tiring trip my heart delights at the sight of my four-legged white friend who seems so pleased to see me.

Bijou is an experienced traveler. He travels first class and sits next to David between his seat and the window. David orders lamb chops for him and gives him ice cubes when he becomes thirsty. He gets jet lag just like the rest of us.

Shamus and Bijou were good friends. They walked together, talked and shared their experiences. Of course Shamus was not as cosmopolitan as his white friend. Dugan and Bijou haven't met yet, so their chemistry is still an unknown quantity. Dogs have definite likes and dislikes, so you can't be sure if they will respond to each other. We've talked about their introduction, so it will come. Also, they both have the same hairdresser. Who knows, they may have already had gossip sessions under the dryer. Their groomer, Mel

Davis, keeps them all day so I feel sure they do communicate between brushings, baths and clippings. In the beginning Dugan barked and acted disagreeable to everyone at Mel's shop; however, his disposition has improved now that he knows what is expected of him. All dogs adore being clean and well-groomed if not the grooming. Mel is special with the dogs; he understands them.

It's a wonderful lazy Sunday in New York City. I slept late and them watched the Virginia Slims Championship tennis finals on T.V. Martina continues to improve her game each year and she took Steffi Graf in three straight sets: 7 - 6 (in a tie breaker), 6 - 4, 6 - 2.

After the tennis was over I took Dugan on a long walk. Each Sunday there is a walking tour guide who brings a group of about thirty people to Beekman Place and gives them a history of the street. Dugan wasn't too pleased to see such a large number of strangers on his block; so he became unusually vocal.

Following our walk I tuned in to see the Giants defeat the Broncos in the last 17 seconds of the game.

The holiday season is upon us. It's a special, lovable season when friends are filled with tender feelings. Traffic becomes more difficult, and people over extend their energy with the added demands. However, I love this time when the Christmas tree goes up in Rockefeller Center. Also, I like the extra luncheons and dinner parties. Usually I stay home on New Year's Eve, but Jan Miner phoned this afternoon to invite me to a formal sit-down dinner for 30. It begins at 10 p.m., a little late for me. I said I would go, but am not sure that I will. She and Dick have great parties, and I enjoy their theatrical friends. It's always a pleasure to get away from the usual group of fashion friends.

As I get older, I find I must pace my energy. It's time consuming to run two households, a demanding job, and write a book at the same time. Even so I get caught up in the excitement of decorating and shopping and feel twice blessed to be able to share the season with those I love.

Thanksgiving is a special holiday and one unique to America. Several times I have been in a foreign country on Thanksgiving, and each time I missed the season of being glad and giving praise for all the fine and beautiful things that the year has brought. It's a time to be in one's home, surrounded by friends and those one loves, a time perhaps to eat and drink good champagne, to sit in front of a lively fire and listen to good music.

This particular Thanksgiving Maya Bowler came from England to spend the weekend at my country mill. It was raining hard and fiercely on the trip up from New York to Connecticut. Peg, my housekeeper, was there to help us into the house with all our food, packages and luggage. Dugan was thrilled to have a long run in the yard, even in the rain.

Peg and I prepared the vegetables, the chicken, the salad and chilled the glasses, while Maya got settled in her room with the large wooden poster bed. After all the chores were done, the three of us met before the living room fire for a bottle of excellent champagne, befitting the season. We laughed and talked and enjoyed the warmth of being cozy inside while the storm continued outside. The more it rained, the louder the sounds were from the stream around the back and side of the mill. Water can be so noisy and immediate. It rises quickly and overflows the stream, but I love the sounds of rushing water. I'm a little afraid of the elements, and at the same time intrigued by their quick excesses.

By Thanksgiving morning the sun was shining, and all seemed right with the whole glorious world. I had not planned to cook on Thursday; so we went to the "Boulder's Inn" in New Preston overlooking the lake, and enjoyed a traditional dinner of the season. This was Maya's first American Thanksgiving and she seemed to enjoy the day.

Friday morning we took Dugan and set out for a sunny day safari. Our first stop was in Washington Depot for lunch at "The Pantry."

This was Dugan's first time to be left alone in the car. I sat at a table where I could keep watch on him while we ate. He was nervous but well-behaved. I ordered and enjoyed a delicious lobster bisque with fresh dill and fresh homemade bread. For dessert I had ginger ice cream. It was very tasty and filled with ginger. Maya did some Christmas shopping at The Pantry and then we headed for Ruth Henderson's silo in the New Milford countryside for more shopping.

Ruth, a friend, was there and it was good to see her again. She had an extra large Christmas tree all decorated with metal cut-outs of animals. It was original, abundant, and appealing. Ruth has a cooking school at the Silo, and she promised to send me one of her favorite recipes as well as a picture of the large, lush tree filled with rocking horses, sheep and cows, and other cute cut-out animals.

Ruth and her husband, Skitch Henderson, conductor of the New York Pop's orchestra, are well known throughout as colorful and original hosts. They have a compound with a number of lovely old houses, the Silo and a dramatic new house built for entertaining. I well remember hiding in the new house, as we waited for Skitch to bring Ruth home for a surprise 50th birthday party.

Ruth was originally from Germany; so she sent me a recipe for German Pancakes (Eierkuchen) and a hot four-berry sauce. She explained that each German state has its own recipe for Eierkuchen. This is the Vogtlandische Art from Ruth's grandmother:

German Pancakes (Eierkuchen)
5 cups flour
1/2 teaspoon salt
12 eggs
5 cups milk
1/2 pound butter, or more as needed

Sift flour in a 5-quart bowl with salt. Make well in center. Beat eggs in a second 5-quart bowl. Add milk and blend. Transfer to a measuring cup.

Pour egg mixture slowly into well while stirring continuously with a mixing spoon. Finish blending with whisk. (Do not use whisk in the beginning because batter is too thick.) Let stand at room temperature for approximately 1 hour. Stir again before using.

Heat a generous ounce (2 tablespoons) butter in a 10-inch omelet pan over high heat. Pour a scant 1/2 C. batter in pan and reduce heat to medium. Cook until golden brown on both sides, turning once. Add more butter to the pan as necessary and wipe out pan if butter begins to burn.

Slide onto a dinner plate. While next Eierkuchen is cooking, roll up the first one and place in a deep 18-inch oven-to-table baking dish. The pancakes must be rolled while still warm and flexible. Continue in this manner until all batter is used. There will be about 24 pancakes.

Cover dish with foil and reheat pancakes in a 250 degree oven before serving. Serves 12.

<u>Hot four-berry Sauce</u>
1/2 lemon with zest
1 1/2 C. sugar, more or less to taste
1 1/2 C. each blackberries, raspberries, currants, or blueberries, and gooseberries, preferably fresh, or frozen or canned. If the berries are canned or frozen in syrup, cook them only with sugar to taste. Drain and rinse fruit canned in syrup, add 1 1/2 ounces good brandy.

Today the weather is gentle, slightly cold, but overflowing with a generous amount of sunshine and the cheer that accompanies the holiday season. When I arrived in Roxbury the leaves were still sprinkled over the yard. Usually Fran Hodges has used his big blower and cleaned them away, as well as cut down the stalks in the garden; however, this year we had two sizable snow falls before Thanksgiving so the leaves were still resting on the lawn waiting for a day so they could be removed. I don't believe in burning the leaves; instead, I use them for fill. They make a rich, moist mulch that is useful.

The Christmas holiday season is upon us. Beekman Place has its own large beautifully decorated tree at the end of 50th Street between Irving Berlin's house and the Korean Embassy. It is silhouetted against the water of the East River.

Today is the day for me to decorate my outside front door. This is the door to my private lobby. Each year I use the same old lacy hanging Christmas scenes. They are hung inside the door so that they hang downward from the individual small window panes. I put on Patsy Kline and then the Judds to use as background music to spur me on. I like these good old country tapes. They give me zest and energy to do a yearly chore. Music makes so many otherwise tiresome jobs a joy. What would we do without a good tape machine and excellent tapes. They take up so much less space than records and also keep better without collecting too much dust.

Gordon Parks has an inventive and creative mind. He seems to do everything he attempts with feeling. This includes his enormous skills as a dramatic and unforgettable cook; therefore, I asked him if he would share one of his favorite recipes with us:

"I've discovered that the imagination I assign to my creative efforts should be no less than that accorded to preparing those palatable dishes my family and friends pretend to have a craving for. Invariably their favorite emerges as one my daughter, Toni, labeled La Cuisine Papa. Now that title recalls a time when our family resided in the south of France; when my children coerced me into transplanting a bit of soul into the everydayness of Frenchly fare. The ingredients put little strain on one's sense of universality. Very simply they are a grandiose mixture of things available in cities, villages and hamlets throughout the universe — chunks of smoked sausage, quarter of white potatoes, green peppers, slices of tomatoes, onions, garlic and a generous portion of flageolets (a green, French version of the American navy bean). Normally all this adds up to — well, sort of trustworthy stew. However, at black-tie time, I often confer dignity upon this culinary delight by dumping it into a large shallow pan, then exposing it to open flames until a crust forms over the surface. Southern style cornbread, a tomato, cucumber and onion salad pontificates the entire potpourri into a "piece de resistance." A good vin blanc, such as Pouilly-Fuisse, renders it superbly digestible.

I'm not sure that this book said any of the things that I meant to say, but I hope, at the very least, that it brought a smile here and there.

The book has been about real people, and about their feelings.

A book never ends, but the time comes to stop writing and to send the manuscript to the publisher. There is no good way to close a book. I so wanted to think of something clever or amusing to say, but nothing came.

During the Christmas season I was watching the Joan Rivers show when the actress Katherine Helmond began talking about her childhood in Texas with her grandmother. Apparently Helmond was a quiet, reticent, shy child who lived a little into herself. She said that she spent her early days with her grandmother who brought her up, and tried to bring her out of herself. One day this tender, colorful grandmother smiled in her gentle way and said, "Laugh, child, ain't nobody getting out of this alive."

I was having a serious discussion with a small boy about the pleasures of nature, and about the mysteries of the elements. It seemed important that I stir his imagination and interest him in the magic and enchantments that surrounded him — to stir the fantasies of an innocent child so that he would see and search out the beauties that waited for him.

Regardless of what age we may be, each one of us is still a child. So I decided to repeat the questions I asked the young boy:

"Where does the wind go?
What happens to melted snow?
Do rivers get tired and stop to rest?
When does Spring get a new dress?"

Twilight has fallen on the garden, and the fairies are dancing.

Fashion Food & Forget-Me-Nots
LaGrange College Alumni
601 Broad Street
LaGrange, Georgia 30240

Please send _____ copies of ***Fashion Food & Forget-Me-Nots*** @ $25.00 each

Ship To:

Name_____

Address_____

City_____State_____Zip_____
Please make checks payable to: ***LaGrange College***

Fashion Food & Forget-Me-Nots
LaGrange College Alumni
601 Broad Street
LaGrange, Georgia 30240

Please send _____ copies of ***Fashion Food & Forget-Me-Nots*** @ $25.00 each

Ship To:

Name_____

Address_____

City_____State_____Zip_____
Please make checks payable to: ***LaGrange College***

Fashion Food & Forget-Me-Nots
LaGrange College Alumni
601 Broad Street
LaGrange, Georgia 30240

Please send _____ copies of ***Fashion Food & Forget-Me-Nots*** @ $25.00 each

Ship To:

Name_____

Address_____

City_____State_____Zip_____
Please make checks payable to: ***LaGrange College***